Machine Learning Fundamentals

Machine Learning Fundamentals

Concepts, Models, and Applications

Rajeev Sahay and Amar Sahay

BEP

BUSINESS EXPERT PRESS

Leader in applied, concise business books

Machine Learning Fundamentals: Concepts, Models, and Applications

Cover design by Brent Beckley

Interior design by Exeter Premedia Services Private Ltd., Chennai, India

First published in 2025 by
Business Expert Press, LLC
222 East 46th Street, New York, NY 10017
www.businessexpertpress.com

ISBN-13: 978-1-63742-748-4 (paperback)
ISBN-13: 978-1-63742-749-1 (e-book)

Business Expert Press Big Data, Business Analytics, and Smart Technology Collection

First edition: 2025

10 9 8 7 6 5 4 3 2 1

EU SAFETY REPRESENTATIVE
Mare Nostrum Group B.V.
Mauritskade 21D
1091 GC Amsterdam
The Netherlands
gpsr@mare-nostrum.co.uk

To Priyanka and Aria, our Love and Joy

Description

Machine Learning Fundamentals provides a comprehensive overview of data science, emphasizing machine learning (ML). This book covers ML fundamentals, processes, and applications, which are used as industry standards. Both supervised and unsupervised learning ML models are discussed.

Topics include data collection and feature engineering techniques as well as regression, classification, neural networks (deep learning), and clustering. Motivated by the success of ML in various fields, this book is designed for a wide audience coming from various disciplines such as engineering, IT, or business and is suitable for those getting started with ML for the first time.

This text can also serve as the main or supplementary text in any introductory data science course from any discipline, offering real-world applications and tools in all areas.

Contents

Preface

Data science is a data-driven decision-making approach that uses several different areas, methods, algorithms, models, and disciplines with the purpose of extracting insights and knowledge from structured and unstructured data. These insights are helpful in applying algorithms and models to make decisions. Data science draws from several fields. The models in data science are used in predictive and prescriptive analytics. Predictive analytics models are used in decision making and predicting future outcomes.

Machine learning (ML) is a key element of data science that uses a set of algorithms to improve predictions and decision making by learning from large quantities of data. With the advancement in storage and computing technologies, an abundance of high-quality data is used efficiently in creating ML models. One of the main reasons for the success of ML applications is the difficulty of applying conventional programming techniques to huge quantities of data. Conventional programming techniques are not able to handle massive amounts of data but are successfully applied in using ML techniques to create and solve numerous problems in different areas ranging from engineering, biological sciences, business, and many more.

The background needed for data science and ML, among other areas, includes the knowledge of linear algebra, statistics and probability, and programming (the most commonly used programming language is Python). This book provides fundamental concepts of ML, managing data and evaluating ML models, the computer packages used in ML, the problem-solving approaches for ML—supervised and unsupervised learning models and their applications, neural networks and deep learning models, training ML models, current state, problems solved using ML, and outlook of the field.

Acknowledgments

We would like to thank the reviewers who took the time to provide excellent insights that helped shape this book.

We greatly appreciate the numerous hours they spent correcting, formatting, and supplying distinctive comments. The book would not be possible without their tireless effort.

We would like to express our gratitude to Prof. Edward Engh, associate professor, for reviewing and administering invaluable suggestions.

Special thanks go to Mr. Anand Kumar, client partner at Tata Consulting Services (TCS), for providing invaluable suggestions. His field and consulting experience in analytical methods greatly helped shape this book.

Thanks to all our students for their input in making this book possible. They have helped us pursue a dream filled with lifelong learning. This book will not be a reality without them.

We are indebted to the senior acquisitions editor, Scott Isenberg; Charlene Kronstedt, director of marketing; and all the reviewers and publishing team at Business Expert Press for their counsel and support during the preparation of this book. We also wish to thank Mark Ferguson, editor, for reviewing the manuscript and providing helpful suggestions for improvement. We greatly appreciate the time he spent correcting, formatting, and supplying distinctive comments.

We acknowledge the help and support of the publishing team for their help with editing and publishing.

We would like to thank our parents who always emphasized the importance of what education brings to the world. Lastly, we would like to express special appreciation to Nilima, Neha, Dave, Smita, Sameer, and Artemis for their creative comments and suggestions. We are grateful for their love, support, and encouragement.

We acknowledge the help and support of Dhinesh, Account Manager at Business Expert Press (BEP) and Kriyadocs Publishing Services, Chennai, India. We thank Dhinesh and his entire team for their help with editing, publishing, and printing.

Introduction

Rajeev Sahay, PhD, Electrical and Computer Engineering (ECE), Asst. Professor, University of California, San Diego (UCSD) Amar Sahay, PhD (Mechanical/Industrial Engineering), Professor, Utah Higher Education

Machine Learning Fundamentals: Concepts, Models, and Applications provides an overview of Data Science with an emphasis in ***Machine Learning (ML)***. With the continued advancement in storage and computing technologies, data science has emerged as one of the most desired fields in driving business and engineering decisions. This book has two major components—data science and ML.

Data science employs techniques and methods from many other fields, such as statistics, mathematics, computer science, engineering, and information science. Besides the methods and theories drawn from several fields, data science uses visualization techniques using specially designed big data software and programming languages, such as Python and R statistical programming.

Data science is a data-driven decision-making approach used to extract knowledge or insights from both structured and unstructured data. The focus of this book is on ML, a key element of Data Science that applies a set of algorithms to improve predictions of business and engineering problems by learning from large quantities of data. ML fundamentals, processes, and steps are discussed in detail. The broad topics the book covers are an introduction to data science, data science and ML frameworks, an overview of ML models, and supervised learning models—regression and classification. The models discussed are univariate and multivariate regression models, logistic regression, neural networks, deep learning frameworks, and several classification models. A separate chapter is dedicated to unsupervised learning models and their applications.

In addition, the other key steps of the ML process such as data collection, data processing, and feature engineering; model training, tuning, and debugging; model evaluation and error analysis of the ML models; and packages used to solve ML problems with applications are discussed.

The book is divided into five different parts with each part divided into chapters that explain the core of data science and ML.

Part 1 of the book introduces the field of data science, the different disciplines it comprises, and the scope with outlook and career prospects. This section also explains ML basics and a brief description of models used in solving various ML problems. The problem formulation, data collection, and exploratory data analysis (EDA) are also discussed. Chapter 3 is about managing data and evaluating ML models.

Part 2: Chapter 4 is devoted to explaining the algorithms and libraries in ML. Chapter 5 deals with working with data. It explains how to get data in the system to build the models.

Chapter 6 deals with supervised learning models. It explains the widely used supervised learning models to solve ML problems.

Part 3 provides a survey of ML methods. Chapter 6 deals with supervised learning models. It explains the widely used supervised learning models to solve ML problems. Among the approaches discussed are supervised and unsupervised learning methods and applications. Under the supervised learning methods, we discuss the linear models—univariate linear regression, multivariate linear regression with n explanatory variables, and logistic regression with binary response variables. Neural networks and their variations, including perceptron—the simplest neural network—neural networks with hidden layers, convolutional neural networks, and recurrent neural networks. Also discussed are the deep learning framework and other supervised ML methods, including K-nearest neighbors, linear and nonlinear support vector machines, decision trees, random forests, and others. Chapter 7 is devoted to unsupervised learning and applications. Among the important models discussed in this category are clustering, k-means, principal component analysis, and anomaly detection. Chapter 8 discusses deep learning models.

Part 4 of the book is devoted to training ML models. This is covered in Chapter 9.

Finally, in Part 5, we discuss the current state and ML state-of-the-art applications. The final chapter discusses the current state of ML and the types of problems ML can solve. It also talks about the future outlook, the continued growth of ML in recent years, and ML as one of the most rewarding careers.

Primary Audience

The book is appropriate for majors in data science, ML, most fields in engineering, analytics, business, graduate students in business and engineering, MBAs, professional MBAs, and working people in business and industry who are interested in learning data science and ML in making effective business decisions. Data science and ML have wide applications that are proven to be effective in predicting future outcomes in a number of engineering and business applications.

The book is designed with a wide variety of audiences in mind. It takes a unique approach to presenting the body of knowledge and integrating such knowledge into different areas of data science and ML. The importance and applications of data science and ML tools in analyzing and solving different problems are emphasized throughout the book. The book also emphasizes basic concepts, models, and applications of ML. It takes a simple yet unique learner-centered approach in presenting the concepts of data science and ML predictive modeling, the knowledge and skills required, as well as the tools. The students in information systems and IT interested in data science will also find the book to be useful.

Scope

This book can be used as a suggested reading for professionals interested in data science, engineering, and business and can also be used as a real-world applications text in data science and ML.

Because of its subject matter and content, the book may also be adopted as a suggested reading in undergraduate and graduate data science, data analytics, ML, statistics, and engineering courses, as well as in MBA and professional MBA courses. The businesses are now data-driven where the decisions are made using real data both collected over time and real-time data. Data science is now an integral part of businesses, and a number of companies rely on data, analytics, business intelligence, ML, and AI applications in making effective and timely business decisions. The professionals involved in data science and analytics, ML, big data, visual analytics, information systems, and business intelligence, as well as business and data analytics, will find this book useful.

PART 1

Data Science and Its Elements

CHAPTER 1

Data Science and Machine Learning (ML)

An Overview and Scope of Data Science

Chapter Highlights

- Introduction
- What Is Data Science?
- Data Science and Associated Fields
- Role of Statistics in Data Science
- Conflicting Definitions of Data Science and Its Relation to Statistics
- A Brief History and Predictions for Data Science
- Data Science and Data Analytics
  - Difference Between Data Science and Data Analytics
- Knowledge and Skills for Data Science Professionals
- Broad View and Data Science Body of Knowledge
- Data Science and Machine Learning (ML)
- Application Areas of Machine Learning (ML)
- Career Path for Data Science Professionals and Data Scientists
- Outlook
- Summary

Introduction

Data science can be viewed as a multidisciplinary field focused on finding actionable insights from large sets of raw, structured, and unstructured data. The field primarily uses different tools and techniques in unearthing answers to the things we don't know. Data science experts use several different areas from statistical analysis, programming, predictive analytics, data visualization, and machine learning (ML) to parse through massive data sets in an effort to observe trends and draw conclusions about data that would not otherwise be inherent.

What Is Data Science?

In this chapter, we explore the field of data science and its relation to ML. Data science is about extracting knowledge and insights from data, while ML, an integral part of data science, is about analyzing, processing, and creating appropriate models from the data to make decisions. Due to its eclectic definition, data science is a multidisciplinary field that involves the applications of several subjects including, but not limited to, statistics, modeling, mathematics, and computer science to address and solve analytically complex problems using data. In this text, we will explore how to use data science in effective ways to make informed data-driven decisions. In doing so, we will draw insights from the several disciplines that intersect with data science.

Data Science may be thought of as a data driven decision making approach that uses different areas, methods, algorithms, models, and disciplines with the purpose of extracting insights and knowledge from structured and unstructured data. The models in data science are used in predictive analytics and machine learning to predict future outcomes.

Data science is applied to extract information from both structured and unstructured data.[1][2] **Unstructured data** is usually not organized and typically contains qualitative or categorical elements, such as dates, categories, and so on, and may also be text-heavy. It also contains numbers and other forms of measurements. The ambiguities in unstructured data make it difficult to apply traditional tools of statistics and data analysis. In recent years, a number of newly developed tools and software programs have emerged that are capable of analyzing big and unstructured data. One of the earliest applications of unstructured data is in analyzing text data using text mining and other methods. **Structured data**, on the other hand, is usually stored in clearly defined fields in databases.

Data scientists' emphasis is on asking the right questions with a goal to seek the right or acceptable solutions. The emphasis is on asking the right questions and not seeking specific answers. This is done by predicting potential *trends*, exploring disparate and disconnected data sources, and finding better ways to analyze information. This typically begins with processing large amounts of unstructured data to be in a structured format. [https://sisense.com/blog/data-science-vs-data-analytics/].

Role of Statistics in Data Science

Data scientists should have a strong background in statistics, mathematics, and general computer programming. Good analytical and statistical skills are a prerequisite to the successful application and implementation of data science tools. Besides the simple statistical tools, data science also uses statistical modeling including descriptive analytics and predictive and prescriptive analytics tools modeling for decision-making and predicting future business outcomes. Thus, a combination of mathematical methods, along with computational algorithms and statistical models, is needed for generating successful data science solutions. Some key statistical concepts that every data scientist should know include:

- Descriptive statistics and data visualization
- Inferential statistics concepts and tools of inferential statistics
- Concepts of probability and probability distributions
- Concepts of sampling and sampling distribution/over- and under-sampling
- Bayesian statistics
- Hypothesis and other inferential procedures

Conflicting Definitions of Data Science and Its Relation to Statistics

Three simplistic and misleading definitions of data science were rejected by Stanford Professor David Donoho. These are (1) data science does not equate to big data, in that the size of the data set is not a criterion to distinguish data science and statistics, (2) data science is not defined by the computing skills of sorting big data sets, in that these skills are already generally used for analyses across all disciplines, and (3) data science is a heavily applied field where academic programs right now do not sufficiently prepare data scientists for the jobs, in that many graduate programs misleadingly advertise their analytics and statistics training as the data science program. [28][29] As a statistician, Donoho, following many in his field, champions the broadening of learning scope in the form of data science [28]. John Chambers urges statisticians to adopt an inclusive concept of learning from data [30]. Together, these statisticians envision an increasingly inclusive applied field that grows out of traditional statistics and beyond.

A Brief History and Predictions for Data Science

The term *data science* was created in the early 1960s to describe a new profession that would support the understanding and interpretation of large amounts of data, which was being amassed at the time [www.data-versity.net/brief-history-data-science/].

The term data science is the result of discussions by scientists, statisticians, researchers, computer scientists, and industry pioneers over the years. Table 1.1 traces the evolution of data science from the 1950s. Needless to say, data science today categorizes a new profession comprising the fields of statistics, applied mathematics, computer science, and programming that provides insights based on large amounts of complex data or big data. The following is a discussion on the evolution of data science that can be traced back to 1957.

In the past 30 years, data science has grown to include businesses and organizations worldwide. It is now being used by governments, geneticists, engineers, and even astronomers. During its evolution, data

Table 1.1

1957	The evolution of data science may be traced back to 1957 when Arthur Samuel coined the term *machine learning* (ML).
1962	John Tukey coined the term *data analysis*. In 1962, he wrote a paper titled "The Future of Data Analysis." He described a shift in the world of statistics and the merging of statistics and computers. John Tucky has several inventions to his name including box plot and exploratory data analysis.
1974	In 1974, Peter Naur used the term *data science* repeatedly in his paper "Concise Survey of Computer Methods." Naur presented his own definition of data science as: "The usefulness of data and data processes derives from their application in building and handling models of reality."
1977	The International Association for Statistical Computing (IASC) was formed. The objectives of the Association are to foster worldwide interest in effective statistical computing and to exchange technical knowledge through international contacts and meetings between statisticians, computing professionals, organizations, institutions, governments, and the general public (https://iasc-isi.org/about-iasc2/).
1986	Carnegie Mellon University Professor Hinton co-authors a paper with David E. Rumelhart and Ronald J. Williams on applying the backpropagation algorithm to multilayer neural networks. This application was a milestone in artificial intelligence (AI) because it allowed the networks to learn internal representations of data.
1989	First data science workshop by the Knowledge Discovery in Databases organization.
1997	In November 1997, C.F. Jeff Wu gave the inaugural lecture entitled "Statistics = Data Science?"[10] for his appointment to the H.C. Carver professorship at the University of Michigan.[11] In this lecture, he characterized statistical work as a trilogy of data collection, data modeling and analysis, and decision-making. In his conclusion, he initiated the modern, noncomputer science, usage of the term *data science* and advocated that statistics be renamed data science and statisticians data scientists.[10] Later, he presented his lecture entitled "Statistics = Data Science?" as the first of his 1998 P.C. Mahalanobis Memorial Lectures.[12]
2001	William S. Cleveland introduced data science as an independent discipline, extending the field of statistics to incorporate "advances in computing with data" in his article "Data Science."
2002	In April 2002, the International Council for Science (ICSU): Committee on Data for Science and Technology (CODATA)[14] started the *Data Science Journal*,[15] a publication focused on issues such

(Continued)

Table 1.1 (Continued)

	as the description of data systems, their publication on the internet, applications, and legal issues.[16]
2003	In January 2003, Columbia University began publishing *The Journal of Data Science*,[17] which provided a platform for all data workers to present their views and exchange ideas. The journal was largely devoted to the application of statistical methods and quantitative research.
2005	The National Science Board published *Long-Lived Digital Data Collections: Enabling Research and Education in the 21st Century* defining data scientists as "the information and computer scientists, database and software and programmers, disciplinary experts, curators and expert annotators, librarians, archivists, and others, who are crucial to the successful management of a digital data collection" whose primary activity is to "conduct creative inquiry and analysis."[18]
2006/2007	Around 2007, Turing Award winner Jim Gray envisioned *data-driven science* as a *fourth paradigm* of science that uses the computational analysis of large data as the primary scientific method[4][5] and "to have a world in which all of the science literature is online, all of the science data is online, and they interoperate with each other."[19]
2012	In the 2012 *Harvard Business Review* article "Data Scientist: The Sexiest Job of the 21st Century,"[20] DJ Patil claims to have coined this term in 2008 with Jeff Hammerbacher to define their jobs at LinkedIn and Facebook, respectively. He asserts that a data scientist is "a new breed," and that a "shortage of data scientists is becoming a serious constraint in some sectors" but describes a much more business-oriented role.
2014	The first international conference: *IEEE International Conference on Data Science and Advanced Analytics* was launched in 2014.[22]
	In 2014, the American Statistical Association (ASA) section on Statistical Learning and Data Mining renamed its journal to *Statistical Analysis and Data Mining: The ASA Data Science Journal*.
2015	In 2015, the *International Journal on Data Science and Analytics*[25] was launched by Springer to publish original work on data science and big data analytics. Google uses Deep Learning to launch speech recognition, Google Voice, and saw a 49% increase in performance. Google launched open-sourced TensorFlow, an AI engine to enact deep learning using big data and cloud.
2016	In 2016, The ASA changed its section name to "Statistical Learning and Data Science."[24]
2017	The DeepMind team released AlphaZero that achieved a superhuman level of play in Chess, Shogi, and Go. PricewaterhouseCoopers (PwC)

(Continued)

Table 1.1 (Continued)

	forecasts job listings for data science and analytics will surge to 2.7 million by 2020.
2020–present	• Data science jobs will increase by around 28% by 2026.
	• The global ML market was valued at $8 billion in 2021 and is anticipated to grow at a 39% compound annual growth rate (CAGR) by 2027.
	• The market for big data analytics in banking could rise to $62.10 billion by 2025.
	• Data creation will grow to more than 180 zettabytes by 2025.
	• Predictions estimate the world will generate 181 zettabytes of data by 2025.
	• [https://onlinestemprograms.wpi.edu/blog/history-data-science-and-pioneers-you-should-know]

science's use of big data was not simply a *scaling up* of the data but included shifting to new systems for processing data and the ways data gets studied and analyzed.

Difference Between Data Science and Data Analytics?

While the terms data science and data analytics are used interchangeably, data science and big data analytics (BDA) are unique fields with the major difference being the scope. Data science is an umbrella term for a group of fields that are used to mine large data sets. Data science has a much broader scope compared to data analytics, analytics, and business analytics. Data analytics is a more focused version of data science and focuses more on data analysis and statistics and can even be considered part of the larger process that uses simple to advanced statistical tools. Analytics is devoted to realizing actionable insights that can be applied immediately based on existing queries.

Another significant difference between the two fields is the question of exploration. Data science isn't concerned with answering specific queries, instead parsing through massive data sets in sometimes unstructured ways to expose insights. Data analysis works better when it is focused, having questions in mind that need answers based on existing data.

Data science produces broader insights that concentrate on which questions should be asked, while BDA emphasizes discovering answers to questions being asked.

More importantly, data science is more concerned with asking questions than finding specific answers. The field is focused on establishing potential trends based on existing data, as well as realizing better ways to analyze and model the data. Table 1.2 outlines the difference between data science and data analytics.

Some argue that the two fields–data science and data analytics–can be considered different sides of the same coin, and their functions are highly interconnected. Data science lays important foundations and parses big data sets to create initial observations, future trends, and potential insights that can be important. This information by itself is useful for some fields, especially modeling, improving ML, and enhancing artificial intelligence (AI) algorithms as it can improve how information is sorted and understood. However, data science asks important questions that we were unaware of before while providing little in the way of answers. By combining data analytics with data science, we have additional insights, prediction capabilities, and tools to apply in practical applications.

When thinking of these two disciplines, it's important to forget about viewing them as data science versus data analytics. Instead, we should see them as parts of a whole that are vital to understanding not just the information we have, but how.

Knowledge and Skills for Data Science Professionals

The key function of the data science professional or a data scientist is to understand the data and identify the correct method or methods that will lead to the desired solution. These methods are drawn from different fields, including data and big data analysis (visualization techniques), statistics (statistical modeling) and probability, computer science and information systems, programming skills, and an understanding of databases, including querying and database management.

Data science professionals should also have knowledge of many of the software packages that can be used to solve different types of

Table 1.2 Difference between data science and data analytics

	Data Science	Data Analytics
Scope	Macro	Micro
Goal	Ask the right questions	Find actionable data
Major fields	ML, AI, search engine engineering, statistics, analytics	Healthcare, gaming, travel, industries with immediate data needs
Analysis of data and big data	Yes	Yes

problems. Some of the commonly used programs are statistical packages (R-statistical computing software), SAS, and other statistical packages; relational database packages (SQL, MySQL, Oracle, and others); and ML libraries (recently, many software programs have emerged to automate ML tasks are available from software vendors). The two known auto ML software are Azur by Microsoft and SAS auto ML.

Broad View of Data Science and Body of Knowledge

Figure 1.1 provides a broader view and key areas of data science. Figure 1.2 outlines the body of knowledge a data science professional is expected to have.

Data Science and Machine Learning (ML)

Data science can be viewed as an umbrella term that constitutes multidisciplinary fields focused on finding actionable insights from large sets of raw, structured, and unstructured data. The field primarily uses different tools and techniques in unearthing answers to the things we don't know (see Figure 1.2). Data science can be viewed as any process or system used to extract knowledge and insights from data. *ML* is one of the key elements of data science. It may be considered a subset of AI. The field of ML can be seen as one of the most important developments in data science. ML focuses on building a set of algorithms designed to find patterns in large data sets (big data). These algorithms are applied to solve various problems by learning from large quantities of data. ML has become very popular because of recent advancements in computing technologies and improved computing and storage capabilities, which make handling, storing, and using vast amounts of data. The other reasons for the successful applications of ML are difficulty and complexity of writing programs for applications like facial recognition that use vast amounts of data. Conventional programming cannot handle huge amounts of data required for facial recognition, stock market predictions, and other applications where real-time dynamic data are needed. The abundance of high-quality data can be used efficiently in ML models. They also improve performance as new data becomes available.

Application Areas of Machine Learning (ML)

ML algorithms are used in a wide variety of applications, such as in engineering, medicine, email filtering, speech recognition, agriculture, computer vision, facial recognition, signal processing, and cyber security to name a few. In these applications, it is difficult or unfeasible to develop conventional algorithms to perform the needed tasks.[3][4] Since the focus of this book is on ML and its applications, we devote Chapter 2 to discuss the details of ML.

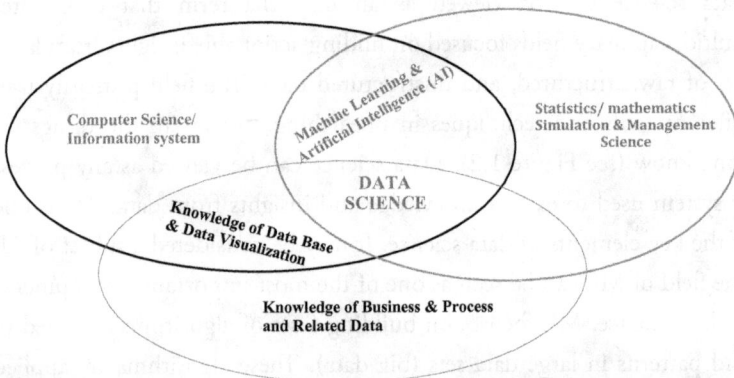

Figure 1.1 Broad view of data science with associated areas

Career Path for Data Science Professionals and Data Scientists

In order to pursue a career in data science, a significant amount of education and experience is required. As evident from Figure 1.2, a data scientist requires knowledge and expertise from varied fields. The field of data science provides a unifying approach by combining varied areas ranging from statistics, mathematics, analytics, business intelligence, computer science, programming, and information systems. It is rare to find a data science professional with knowledge and background in all these areas. It is often the case that a data scientist has specialization in a subfield. The minimum education requirement for a data science professional is a bachelor's degree in mathematics, statistics, or computer science. A number of data scientists possess a master's or a PhD degree in data science with adequate experience in the field. The application of data science tools varies depending on the field it is applied to. Note that data science tools and applications when applied to engineering may be different from computer science or business. Therefore, the successful application of tools of data science requires expertise and knowledge of the process. Because of the recent boom and interest in data science, ML, and AI, many universities are now offering degrees and/or specializations in data science and ML ranging from undergraduate to graduate degrees.

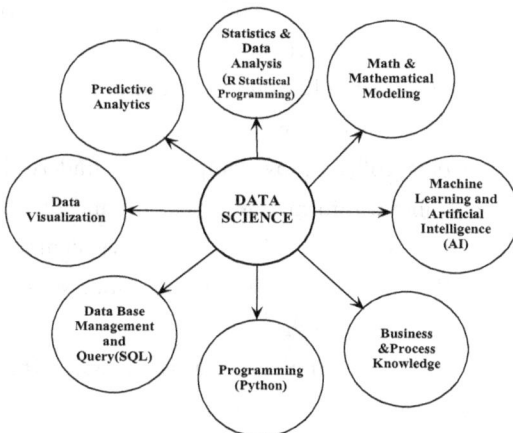

Figure 1.2 Data science body of knowledge

Outlook

Data science is a growing field. It continues to evolve as one of the most sought-after areas by companies. A career in data science is ranked as the third-best job in America for 2020 by Glassdoor and was ranked the number-one-best job from 2016 to 2019.[29] Data scientists have a median salary of $118,370 per year or $56.91 per hour.[30] These are based on level of education and experience in the field. Job growth in this field is also above average, with a projected increase of 16 percent from 2018 to 2028.[3] The largest employer of data scientists in the USA is the federal government, employing 28 percent of the data science workforce. Other large employers of data scientists are computer system design services, research and development laboratories, big technology companies, and colleges and universities. Typically, data scientists work full-time, and some work more than 40 hours a week.[3]

The outlook for the data science field looks promising. It is estimated that 2.5–2.0 million jobs will be created in this area in the next 10 years. The data science area is vast and requires knowledge and training from different fields. It is one of the fastest-growing areas. Data scientists can have a major positive impact on a business' success.

Data science continues to evolve as one of the most promising and in-demand career paths for skilled professionals. Today, successful data professionals understand that they must advance past the traditional skills of analyzing large amounts of data, data mining, and programming skills. In order to uncover useful intelligence for their organizations, data scientists must master the full spectrum of the data science life cycle and possess a level of flexibility and understanding to maximize returns at each phase of the process.

Much of the data collected by companies is underutilized. These data, through meaningful information extraction and discovery, can be used to make critical business decisions and drive significant business change. It can also be used to optimize customer success and subsequent acquisition, retention, and growth.

Business and research treat their data as an asset. The businesses, processes, and companies are run using their data. The data and variables collected are highly dynamic and continuously change. Data science professionals are needed to process, analyze, and model the data, which are usually in the big data form to be able to visualize and help companies in making timely data-driven decisions. Data science professionals must be trained to understand, clean, process, and analyze the data to extract value from it. It is also important to be able to visualize the data using conventional and big data software in order to communicate data in a meaningful way. This will enable applying proper statistical, modeling, and programming techniques to be able to draw conclusions. All these require knowledge and skills from different areas, and these are hugely important skills in the next decades."— Hal Varian, chief economist at Google and UC Berkeley professor of information sciences, business, and economics.[3] The increase in demand for data science jobs is expected to grow by 28 percent by 2020 [https://datascience.berkeley.edu/about/what-is-data-science/]. The following are some recent statistics on data science and data analytics: [https://techjury.net/blog/big-data-statistics/]

- Data science jobs will increase by around 31 percent by 2031(*Source: Towards Data Science*).
- The BDA market is set to reach $103 billion by 2023.
- The demand for composite data analytics professionals will grow by 31 percent by 2030 (*Source: Forbes*).
- Estimates by the U.S. Bureau of Labor point to a 31 percent growth come 2030. Composable analytics will be at the forefront of adoption, with 60 percent of organizations embracing it because of the cost reduction benefit.
- According to Wikibon, the BDA market is expected to reach $49 billion with a compounded annual growth rate (CAGR) of 11 percent by 2025. So, each year, the market will gain $7 billion in value. According to this forecast, the BDA market should reach $103 billion by the end of the prediction period.
- Ninety-six percent of companies plan to hire job seekers with big data skills (*Source: The Economic Times*).

Summary

Data science is a data-driven decision-making approach that uses several areas, methods, algorithms, models, and disciplines with the purpose of extracting insights and knowledge from structured and unstructured data. These insights are helpful in applying algorithms and models to make decisions.

The chapter explores data science and its associated areas. Data science as a multidisciplinary field involves the applications of several subjects including, but not limited to, statistics, modeling, mathematics, and computer science to address and solve analytically complex problems using data. The field has a close relation to statistical modeling and programming.

This chapter provided an overview of data science by defining and outlining the tools and techniques and explained the differences and similarities between data science and data analytics. Data science continues to evolve as one of the most sought-after areas by companies. The chapter provided a brief history of data science and outlined the career path and job outlook for this area which continues to be one of the highest of all fields. The field is promising and is showing tremendous job growth. ML as one of the key elements of data science was discussed briefly. The field of ML can be seen as one of the most important developments in data science.

CHAPTER 2

Introduction and Basics of Machine Learning (ML)

- What Is Machine Learning?
- Why Machine Learning?
- Machine Learning Problem Solving Approach
- Supervised Learning
- Unsupervised Learning
- Difference between Supervised and Unsupervised Learning
- Overview of Machine Learning Models
  - Regression
    - Simple and Multiple Regression
    - Other Types of Regression Models
- Classification
  - Difference between Classification and Regression
  - Different Types of Classification tasks in Machine Learning
    - Binary Classification
    - Multi-class Classification Commonly Used Classification Algorithms
  - Logistic Regression
  - Naïve Bayes'
  - Support Vector Machines (SVM)
    - Types of SVMs
  - K-nearest Neighbor
  - Random Forest Algorithm
  - Neural Networks
  - Deep Learning

- Unsupervised Learning
- Common Unsupervised Learning Approaches

- Clustering
- Types of Clustering Methods
  - o K-Means Clustering
  - o Divisive Clustering
  - o Mean Shift Clustering Algorithm
  - o Gaussian Mixture Model
- Association Rules
- Dimensionality Reduction
- Semi-supervised Machine Learning
- Reinforcement Learning
- Evaluation Metrics for Regression Models
- Some Fundamental Concepts Related to Machine Learning
- Summary

What Is Machine Learning (ML)?

ML is a method of designing systems that can learn, adjust, and improve based on the data fed to them without being explicitly programmed. ML applications are a way of analyzing and creating models from a very large sample or huge amounts of data commonly referred to as *big data*. ML is closely related to artificial intelligence (AI). In fact, it is an application of AI.

Why Machine Learning?

The ML approach is used because conventional programming, in many cases, cannot handle the huge quantity of data and problems at hand. For simple tasks, it is not difficult to develop a program and instruct the computer to execute the steps and tasks that can solve the problem. In these cases, no learning is needed. For more advanced and complex tasks, it may be challenging to write programs to execute the required tasks because of huge quantities of data and the complexity of the task. In such cases, it seems more logical and effective to program the machine to develop and learn from its own algorithms. Some examples where machines can be used to develop their own algorithms and not depend on programmers to execute the steps needed are programming facial recognition or stock market predictions. *[17]*—Alpaydin, Ethem. *Introduction to Machine Learning,* 4th ed. (MIT, 2020). xix, 1–3, 13–18. ISBN 978-0262043793.

In ML applications, huge amounts of data are needed, and it is challenging to develop programs to accomplish the task due to many potential answers. One approach used in such cases is to label some correct answers as valid answers and use this as ***training data.*** Using the training data, the computer improves the algorithms to find the correct answer.

Machine Learning Problem-Solving Approach

At the fundamental level, ML tasks are typically classified into following broad categories depending on the nature of the problem and learning *signal* or *feedback* available to a learning system. These are [20]

1. Supervised learning
2. Unsupervised learning
3. Semisupervised learning
4. Reinforced learning

The broad categories of ML are explained in Figure 2.1.

Supervised Learning

In supervised learning, the computer is presented with example inputs and their desired outputs by the analyst, and the goal is to create a model to learn a general rule that maps inputs to outputs. The learning

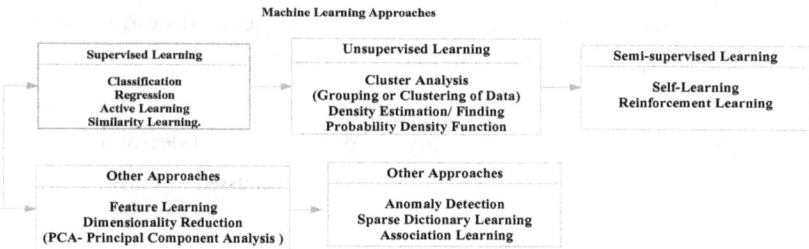

Machine Learning Approaches

Supervised Learning	Unsupervised Learning	Semi-supervised Learning
Classification Regression Active Learning Similarity Learning.	Cluster Analysis (Grouping or Clustering of Data) Density Estimation/ Finding Probability Density Function	Self-Learning Reinforcement Learning
Other Approaches	Other Approaches	
Feature Learning Dimensionality Reduction (PCA- Principal Component Analysis)	Anomaly Detection Sparse Dictionary Learning Association Learning	

Figure 2.1 Types of machine learning problems and approaches

involves creating a model by establishing the relationship between inputs or the *features* and the desired output or some *label*. Once this model is established, it can be used to apply labels to new, unknown data to predict future events. The idea is to learn from the past data and apply it to new data to make predictions for future events using the created learning algorithm.

In supervised learning, there is a set of measurements (x_i, y_i) where x_i are the input or predictor measurements and y_i are the corresponding response values. Thus, for each observation of the predictor measurement(s) $x_i, i = 1, 2, ..., n$, there is a corresponding associated measurement of the response variable, $y_i; = 1, 2, ..., n$. We fit a model that relates the response to predictors. The fitted model is used to predict the response for future values. Commonly used models in this category include linear regression, logistic regression, and several others. These models are discussed in Chapter 6.

Unsupervised Learning

In unsupervised learning, no labels are given to the program. Unsupervised learning is where we have only input data (x_i) and no corresponding output variables. The learning algorithm is expected to find the structure in its input. The goal of unsupervised learning is to find hidden patterns in the large data. For example, suppose we have n measurements, $x_i, i = 1, 2, 3, ..., n$, but no corresponding response measurements, y_i. In this case, it is not possible to fit a regression model, since there is no response variable. This is the case of unsupervised learning where there is no response to predict. In such cases, prediction is not an objective, rather we try to understand the relationships between the variables or between the measurements. Instead of making predictions, we may be interested to determine whether the measurements fall into distinct groups. This is commonly known as *cluster analysis*, which is a commonly used unsupervised learning model. Additional unsupervised learning models are discussed in Chapter 6.

Table 2.1 Difference between supervised and unsupervised learning

Supervised Learning	Unsupervised Learning
Supervised learning uses a set of input variables $(x_1, x_2, ..., x_n)$ and an output variable, $y(x)$. An algorithm of the form $y = f(x)$ is used to learn the mapping function relating the input to output. Note that inputs are also known as features and the output is referred to as the target.	Unsupervised learning uses a set of input variables but not output variables. No labels are given to the learning algorithm. The algorithm is expected to find the structure in its input. The goals of unsupervised learning may be finding hidden patterns in the large data or feature learning. Thus, unsupervised learning can be a goal in itself or a means toward an end that is not based on general rules of teaching and training the algorithms.
This mapping function or the model relating the input and output variable is used to predict the output variable. The goal is to obtain the mapping function that is so accurate that it can use even the new set of data, that is, the model can be used to predict the output variable as the new data becomes available.	Unlike supervised learning, unsupervised algorithms are designed to devise and find an interesting structure in the data.
The name supervised learning means that in this process the algorithm is trained to learn from the training data set where the learning process is supervised. In a supervised learning process, the expected output or the answer is known. The algorithm is designed to make predictions iteratively from the training data and is corrected by the analyst as needed. The learning process stops when the algorithm provides the desired level of performance and accuracy.	The most used unsupervised learning problems are clustering and association problems.
	In clustering, a set of inputs is to be divided into groups. Unlike classification, the groups are not known beforehand, making this typically an unsupervised task.
The most used supervised problems are regression and classification problems. We briefly mentioned regression problems earlier. Time series prediction problems, random forest for classification and regression problems, and support vector machines for classification problems also fall in this category.	**Association:** association problems are used to discover rules that describe association such as people that buy X also tend to buy Y.

Difference Between Supervised and Unsupervised Learning

The difference between supervised and unsupervised learning is further explained in Table 2.1.

Overview of Machine Learning Models

ML uses a vast set of tools for understanding data and solving problems. Here we will briefly discuss the supervised learning models followed by the unsupervised algorithms.

Supervised learning problems can be divided into two main categories: (1) *regression* **and** (2) *classification problems*. The details of the **supervised learning** models are outlined in Figure 2.2.

Supervised learning refers to building models used for predicting an output using one or more input variables. This type of problem appears in several fields ranging from business, engineering, medicine, physics, astronomy, and others. Supervised learning problems fall into two broad categories—**regression** and **classification**.

Regression

Regression analysis is one of the widely used supervised learning models. The method is used to identify the relationship between a dependent variable and one or more independent variables and is used to make predictions about future outcomes. When there is only one independent variable and one dependent variable, it is known as a simple linear regression. As the number of independent variables

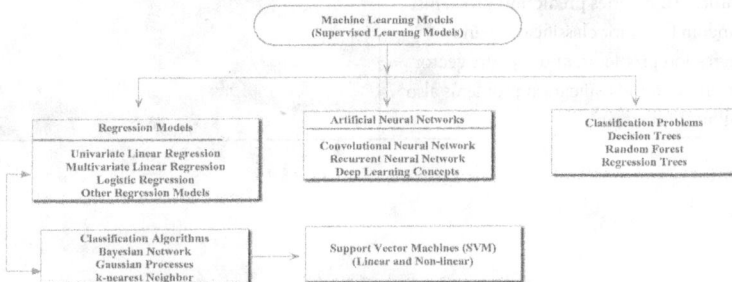

Figure 2.2 Supervised machine learning models

increases, it is referred to as multiple linear regression. For a simple linear regression, it tries to fit a line of best fit, which is calculated using the method of least squares. There are many other types of regression models. Regression is one of the widely used supervised learning models. Regression is a supervised problem where the outputs are continuous rather than discrete. Some examples of regression problems are predicting sales using advertisement expenditure, predicting the mileage of a car, predicting, demand, and so on.

Regression analysis is used to study and explain the mathematical relationship between two or more variables and predict one variable using the other variable or variables. By mathematical relationship, we mean whether the relationship between the variables is linear or nonlinear. Sometimes we may be interested in only two variables. In regression, the variable to be predicted is known as the dependent variable and the other variable is independent variable. The input variable is usually denoted by X. There may be more than one input variable. In this case, they are denoted using a subscript written as $X_1, X_2, ..., X_n$. The input variables go by different names, such as **predictors, independent variables**, or *features*. These terms are used interchangeably. The output variable is called the **dependent variable, response variable, or target** and is often denoted using the symbol, Y.

Suppose we are interested in the relationship between sales and advertising. Companies spend millions of dollars on advertising and expect that an increase in advertising expenditure will significantly improve sales. Thus, these two variables might be related. Other examples where two variables might be related are production cost and the volume of production, increase in summer temperature and the home heating cost, or the size of house in square feet and its price. Once the relationship between two variables is established, we can predict one variable using the other variable or variables. For example, if we can establish a relationship between the sales and advertising, we can predict the sales y using advertising expenditure x. This can be done using a mathematical relationship between the sales and advertising as

$$Y = f(x) + \varepsilon$$

In many cases, there may be n independent variables or predictors, $X_1, X_2, ..., X_n$. In this case, the relationship between the response Y and the predictors $(X_1, X_2, ..., X_n)$ can be written as

$$Y = f(X) + \varepsilon$$

This is an example of a **supervised learning model** as the problem can be modeled to predict an output variable, for example, sales based on advertising cost—an input variable.

Simple and Multiple Regression Models

When there are only two variables involved—one response and a single predictor variable, the relationship is explained and studied using the technique of **simple regression analysis**. Many problems involve situations where many variables are involved. In such cases, we are interested in predicting one variable using several variables. The problem involving many variables is studied using the technique of **multiple regression analysis** where we are interested in predicting one variable using several input variables.

The objective in simple regression is to predict one variable using the other variable. The variable to be predicted is known as the **dependent** or **response** variable or the **target** and the other variable is known as the **independent** variable, **feature**, or **predictor**. Thus, the problem of simple regression involves one dependent and one independent variable. An example would be to predict the sales (the dependent variable) using the advertising expenditure (the independent variable). In multiple regression problems, where the relationship between multiple variables is of interest, the objective is to predict one variable—the dependent variable using the other variables known as independent variables. An example of multiple regression would be to predict the sales for a grocery chain using the food item sales, nonfood item sales, size of the store, and the operating hours (12 or 24 hours). *The multiple regression problem involves one dependent and two or more independent variables.* In regression, the target variable is continuous. The other commonly used regression algorithms are logistic regression and polynomial regression.

Other Regression Models

There are several regression models used in ML. The commonly used regression algorithms are as follows:

1. Ordinary least squares regression (OLSR)
2. Linear regression/multiple regression
3. Logistic regression
4. Ridge regression
5. Nonlinear regression
6. Lasso regression and others

Classification

Classification is another type of supervised learning problem. Classification algorithms assign test data into specific categories. The prediction task is a *classification* when the target variable is discrete. In classification, the labels are discrete categories where the inputs are divided into two or more classes, and the learner must produce a model that assigns unseen inputs to one or more (multilabel classification) of these classes. For example, a financial institution may study the potential of borrowers to predict whether a group of new borrowers may be classified as having a high degree of risk. Spam filtering is another example of classification, where the inputs are email messages that are classified into classes as *spam* and *no spam*.

Classification algorithms categorize the new data according to the observations of the training set. *Classification is a supervised learning technique* where a training set is used to find similarities in classes. This means that the input data are divided into two or more classes or categories and the learner creates a model that assigns inputs to one or more of these classes. The objects are classified based on the training set of data. In a classification problem, the output variable is a category, such as emails can be classified as *spam* or *no spam* or a test can be classified as *negative* and *positive*. The algorithm that implements classification is known as the classifier. Some of the most commonly used classification algorithms are **K-NN** algorithm, decision **Tree** algorithms, and others discussed in subsequent sections.

Classification can also be seen as a predictive modeling problem where a class label is predicted for a given set of input data, for example, the algorithm may be designed to classify whether given handwritten characters is one of the known characters.

While both classification and regression are prediction problems, there are differences between them. Table 2.2 outlines the differences.

Different Types of Classification Tasks in Machine Learning

Some common classification tasks in ML are binary and multiclass classification.

Binary Classification

In a binary classification, the objective is to classify the input data into two mutually exclusive categories. The training data are labeled in a binary format: true and false; positive and negative; 0 and 1; spam and not spam; and so on, depending on the type of problem. For instance, we might want to detect whether a given image is a truck or a boat.

MultiClass Classification

The multiclass classification algorithms have at least two mutually exclusive class labels, and the objective here is to predict to which class a given input example belongs. For example, from the given images of boats, planes, and cars, the model is required to classify the correct image.

Commonly Used Binary Classification Algorithms

Most of the binary classification algorithms can also be used for multiclass classification. The commonly used classification algorithms are:

Table 2.2 **Difference between classification and regression models**

	Classification	Regression
1	Used to predict discrete target variables. The classification algorithm is used to classify a new instance into one of the two categories *yes* or *'no.*	The regression problems predict the continuous variables. The target variable is continuous.
2	The algorithm tries to find the best possible decision boundary that separates the two classes with the maximum possible separation.	In the simple linear regression algorithm, we try to find the best-fit line or plane that represents a mathematical expression relating the target variable and the features.

3.	The model evaluation is done using:
	• Classification accuracy (which is the ratio of correct prediction divided by total number of input samples). The percentage gives the model accuracy.
	
	• Logarithmic loss or log loss. It works by penalizing the false (false positive) classification.
	
	• Area under curve: it is one of the widely used metrics used for binary classification.
	
	• F1 score: F1-scores are used to evaluate the performance of the classification algorithms. This metric usually tells us about the precision. The important metrics are:
	  ○ Precision
	
	  ○ Recall
	
	• Confusion matrix
		The model performance is done using metrics like mean squared error (MSE), coefficient of determination, R^2, and MAPE. These are used to evaluate the performance of the regression models.

4.	The classification problems are binary classification or multiclass classification problems.	Regression problems are simple regression, multiple regression, ridge regression, nonlinear regression models, and their variations.

(Continued)

Table 2.2 (Continued)

	Classification	Regression
5	Objective is to predict categorical/class labels.	Objective is to predict continuous numerical target.
6	Examples in this case are spam detection, image recognition, sentiment analysis, and disease characterization.	Examples are predicting profit, sales, or demand for a company, stock price prediction, predicting home price, stock value prediction, forecasting demand.

- Logistic regression
- Naïve Bayes
- SVM
- K-nearest neighbors (K-NN)
- Neural networks
- Deep learning

Logistic regression: the linear regression is used when dependent variables are continuous, whereas logistic regression is the appropriate model when the dependent variable is categorical, that is they have binary outputs, such as *true* and *false* or *yes* and *no*. While both regression models are applied to understand the relationships between inputs and output, logistic regression is mainly used to solve binary classification problems, such as spam identification.

Naïve Bayes: Naïve Bayes or a Naïve Bayes classifier is a probabilistic ML model that is used for classification task. The classifier is based on the Bayes' theorem. These classifiers are a collection of classification algorithms where all of them share a common principle, that is, every pair of features being classified is independent of each other.

Types of Naïve Bayes Classifier

Multinomial Naïve Bayes: one of the common applications of this classifier is in document classification problem, that is, whether a document belongs to the category of technology, finance, sports, politics, and so on. The features or the predictors used by this classifier are the frequency of words present in the document.

Bernoulli Naïve Bayes: in this classifier, the predictors are binary meaning the parameters used to predict the class variable take up only values *yes* or *no*, for example, if a word occurs in the text or not.

Gaussian Naïve Bayes: in this case, the predictors are continuous with an assumption that the values have a Gaussian distribution.

Some of the applications of Naïve Bayes algorithms are sentiment analysis, spam filtering, recommendation systems, and so on. These algorithms are simple and easy to implement. The limitation of this algorithm is the assumption that the features or predictors are independent, which may not be the case in real-world situations. This technique is primarily used in text classification, spam identification, and recommendation systems.

Support Vector Machines (SVM)

A SVM is a ML algorithm that uses supervised learning algorithms to solve classification, regression, and outlier detection problems. The method is widely used for classification problems. The method works by performing optimal data transformation creating a hyperplane separating the two classes of data where the distance between two classes of data points is at its maximum. The main objective of the SVM algorithm is to identify a hyperplane that distinguishes and segregates the data points of different classes. SVMs have wide applications in health care, natural language processing, signal processing applications, and speech and image recognition fields.

Types of Support Vector Machines

SVMs can be classified as simple or linear SVM and kernel or nonlinear SVM.

1. Simple or linear SVM
   o Linear SVMs are used to classify linearly separable data. When a data set can be segregated into categories or classes using a single straight line, it is known as a linear SVM classifier. In this case, data are linearly distinct or separable. A simple SVM is typically used to address classification and regression analysis problems.
2. Kernel or nonlinear SVM
   o When the data cannot be segregated into distinct categories using a straight line, then the nonlinear classification using a kernel or nonlinear SVM can be used. This type of classifier is referred to as a nonlinear classifier. In this case, the classification can be performed with a nonlinear data type by adding features into higher dimensions rather than a 2D space. The added features fit a hyperplane that helps easily separate classes or categories. Kernel SVMs are used to handle optimization problems with multiple variables. SVMs methods classify unknown data into known categories. They have applications in diverse fields. Some of the application areas include facial detection and expression classification, text categorization and handwriting recognition, and speech recognition. Some other areas where SVMs find applications are text categorization handwriting recognition and speech recognition.

The K-Nearest Neighbor

The K-NN algorithm is a nonparametric supervised learning algorithm. It is a popular ML technique used for classification and regression tasks but mainly for classification. The K in KNN is a parameter that determines the number of nearest neighbors to include in the process. It is considered a nonparametric method because it does not make any assumptions about the distribution of underlying data. The KNN algorithm tries to determine to what group a data point belongs to by looking at the data points around it.

It uses proximity to make classifications or predictions about the grouping of an individual data point. The algorithm assumes that similar data points can be found near each other, and based on this assumption, it calculates the distance between data points using Euclidean distance (the most preferred distance calculation method), and then it assigns a category based on the most frequent category or average.

Its ease of use and low processing time make it a preferred algorithm, but as the test data set grows, the processing time increases making it less attractive for classification tasks. KNN is typically used for recommendation engines and image recognition.

Random Forest Algorithm

Random forest is an ML algorithm that combines the output of multiple decision trees to reach a single result. It is used for both classification and regression problems. A decision tree is an algorithm used to classify data. It is like a probability tree that draws a clear pathway to a decision or outcome. It is a single starting point that branches off into two or more directions, with each branch of the tree showing different possible outcomes.

Random forest grows multiple decision trees which are merged for a more accurate prediction.

The logic behind the random forest model is that it uses multiple uncorrelated decision trees that perform much better as a group than they do alone. When using random forest for classification, each tree provides a classification or a *vote*. The algorithm chooses the classification with the majority votes. In the case of random forest for regression, the forest picks the average of the outputs of all trees.

The regression and classification algorithms are discussed in detail in Chapter 6.

Neural Networks

Neural networks are also known as artificial neural networks (ANNs) and are comprised of node layers with an input layer, weights, a bias (or threshold), one or more hidden layers, and an output layer.

Each node or neuron is connected to another and has an associated weight and threshold. If the output of an individual node is above the specified threshold value, that node is activated and sends data to the next layer of the network. Otherwise, no data are passed along to the next layer of the network.

Neural networks rely on training data to learn and improve their accuracy over time. Modern neural networks are nonlinear statistical data modeling tools. They are usually used to model complex relationships between inputs and outputs and to find patterns in data. Some applications of neural networks are found in speech recognition or image recognition. One of the most well-known neural networks is Google's search algorithm.

In ML, neural networks have wide applications in **deep learning**. Deep learning is a subset of ML, which is essentially a neural network with three or more layers. A simple neural network is shown in Figure 2.3.

Deep Learning [8]

Deep learning is a class of ML algorithms based on ANNs. Here the learning can be supervised, semisupervised, or unsupervised.[2]

Falling hardware prices and the development of GPUs for personal use in the last few years have contributed to the development of the concept of deep learning, which consists of multiple hidden layers in an ANN. This approach tries to model the way the human brain processes light and sound into vision and hearing. Some successful applications of deep learning are computer vision and speech recognition.

Deep learning uses multiple layers to progressively extract higher-level features from the input.

Deep-learning architectures include deep neural networks, deep belief networks, deep reinforcement learning (RL), recurrent neural networks, convolutional neural networks, and transformers. These have

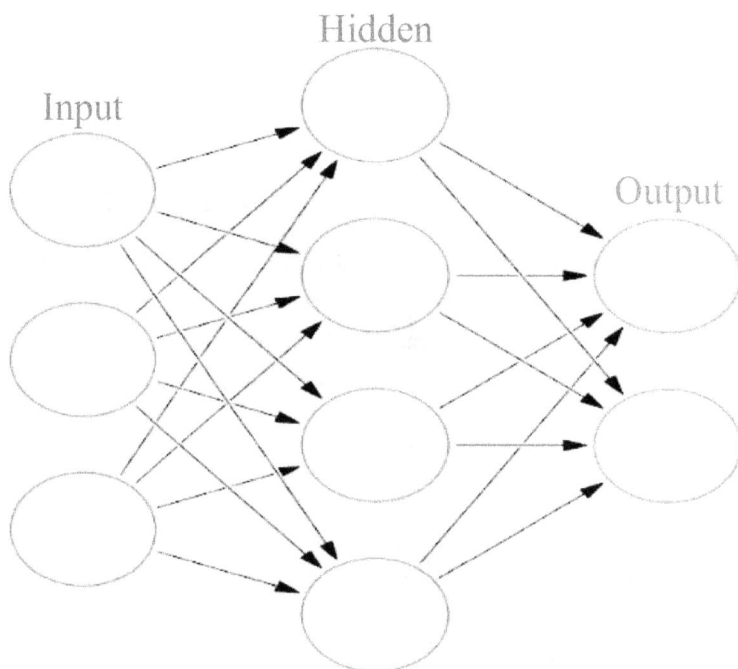

Figure 2.3 A simple neural network

been applied to fields including computer vision, speech recognition, natural language processing, machine translation, bioinformatics, drug design, medical image analysis, climate science, material inspection, and board game programs, where they have produced results comparable to and in some cases surpassing human expert performance.[3][4][5]all are 27 in Reference

Chapter 8 provides details of deep learning.

Unsupervised Learning

Unsupervised learning is a class of problems where there are inputs but no outputs or labels. Here are some examples to better understand the supervised and unsupervised learning models.

Unsupervised learning ML algorithms are used to analyze and cluster *unlabeled* data sets. These algorithms find hidden patterns or groupings in the data without the need for human intervention. The unsupervised algorithms have applications in exploratory data analysis, customer segmentation, image processing, knowledge discovery in data, and many others.

Common Unsupervised Learning Approaches

Unsupervised learning models are used for three main tasks—**clustering**, **association**, and **dimensionality reduction**. These are discussed in the following with associated algorithms and approaches.

Clustering

Clustering is an unsupervised learning algorithm. Unlike supervised learning, the input is not labeled and problem solving is based on the experience that the algorithm gains by solving similar problems as a training schedule.

Clustering groups of unlabeled data based on their similarities or differences. Clustering algorithms are used to process raw, unclassified data objects into groups represented by structures or patterns in the information.

Clustering organizes similar objects into groups in many **ML** applications. Clustering has applications across various fields, such as marketing where clustering can be used to segment customers based on their buying patterns. This information can be used for promotion and advertising.

Types of Clustering Methods

In clustering, the formation of clusters uses several criteria. They use different parameters like shortest distance, graphs, and density of the data points. Grouping into clusters may be based on similarity measurements. There are different types of clustering approaches. They use different methods to group the data from the data sets. This section describes the clustering approaches. Some clustering methods and their applications are discussed here.

Clustering algorithms can be categorized into a few types, specifically exclusive, overlapping, hierarchical, and probabilistic.

Exclusive and Overlapping Clustering

Exclusive clustering is a form of grouping that stipulates a data point can exist only in one cluster. This can also be referred to as *hard* clustering. The K-means clustering algorithm is an example of exclusive clustering.

K-Means Clustering

k-means is the most widely used centroid-based clustering algorithm. Centroid-based algorithms are efficient but sensitive to initial conditions and outliers. This is an efficient, effective, and simple clustering algorithm.

A common example of an exclusive clustering method is where data points are assigned into K groups where K is the number of clusters based on the distance from each group's centroid. The data points closest to a given centroid will be clustered under the same category. A larger K value will be indicative of smaller groupings, whereas a smaller K value will have a larger grouping. K-means clustering is commonly used in market segmentation, document clustering, image segmentation, and image compression.

K-means is a partition-based clustering technique that uses Euclidean distances between the points as a criterion for the formation of clusters. K-means groups *n* number of data points into a predetermined *k* number of clusters. A center is allocated to each cluster and each cluster is placed at farthest distance. The incoming data point is placed in a cluster with the closest cluster center. This process of placing the data points is repeated until all the data points get assigned to a cluster. After all the data points are allocated into clusters, the cluster centers or centroids are recalculated. Once the *k* new centroids are found, a new grouping is done between the nearest new centroid and the same data set points. The process is an iterative approach that may lead to a different k centroid value and their location. The iteration continues until the cluster centers do not change or the centroids do not move anymore.

Hierarchical Clustering

Hierarchical clustering, also known as connectivity-based clustering. This unsupervised clustering algorithm is based on the principle that every object is connected to its neighbors depending on their proximity distance (degree of relationship). The clusters are represented in extensive hierarchical structures separated by a maximum distance required to connect the cluster parts. The clusters are represented as **Dendrograms**, where X-axis represents the objects that do not merge, while Y-axis is the distance at which clusters merge. The similar data objects have minimal distance falling in the same cluster, and the dissimilar data objects are placed farther in the hierarchy. Mapped data objects correspond to a cluster amid discrete qualities concerning the multidimensional scaling, quantitative relationships among data variables, or cross-tabulation in some respects. The hierarchical clustering may vary in the data flow chosen in the following categories.

Hierarchical clustering can be categorized in two ways: agglomerative or divisive.

Agglomerative clustering is considered a *bottoms-up approach*. Its data points are isolated as separate groupings initially then they are merged iteratively on the basis of similarity until one cluster has been achieved. Four different methods are commonly used to measure similarity.

Ward's linkage: in this method, the distance between two clusters is defined by the increase in the sum of squares after the clusters are merged.

Average linkage: this method is defined by the mean distance between two points in each cluster.

Complete (or maximum) linkage: this method is defined by the maximum distance between two points in each cluster.

Single (or minimum) linkage: this method is defined by the minimum distance between two points in each cluster.

Euclidean distance is the most common metric used to calculate these distances; however, other metrics, such as Manhattan distance, are also cited in clustering literature.

Divisive clustering can be defined as the opposite of agglomerative clustering. It takes a *top-down* approach where all the data points belong to one large cluster and tries to divide the data into smaller groups based on a termination logic or a point beyond which there will be no further division of data points.

Mean Shift Clustering Algorithm

Mean shift clustering is a nonparametric, simple, and flexible clustering technique. It is based on estimated distribution of a given data set known as kernel density estimation. The basic principle of the algorithm is to assign the data points to the specified clusters recursively by shifting points toward the peak or highest density of data points. It is used in the image segmentation process.

Gaussian Mixture Model

The Gaussian mixture model (GMM) is a distribution-based clustering technique. It assumes that the data follows a Gaussian distribution. In this method of clustering, the probability of a point being a part of a cluster is inversely dependent on distance. This means that as the distance from distribution increases, the probability of a point belonging to the cluster decreases.

GMM determines probabilities and allocates them to data points in the K number of clusters. Each of which has three parameters: mean, covariance, and mixing probability. To compute these parameters, GMM uses the expectation maximization technique.

Some of the applications of clustering are in market segmentation, retail marketing and sales, wireless network analysis, network traffic classification, regulating streaming services, health care, and others.

In summary, clustering is an unsupervised method that takes a huge amount of unlabeled input data and clusters them as a group based on of some similarity metrics.

There are several clustering methods. Some are explained above. The best method is selected based on the available data set and application.

The main cluster analysis techniques are centroid-based/partition clustering, hierarchical-based clustering, distribution-based clustering, and density-based clustering.

Association

Association is another type of unsupervised learning method that uses different rules to find relationships between variables in a given data set. It is **a technique used to uncover hidden relationships between variables in large data sets**. This is a commonly used ML algorithm that has a wide range of applications in various fields. Some of the common applications of association rules are in market basket analysis, customer segmentation, and fraud detection. Association rules are useful for analyzing and predicting customer behavior. For example, "Customers who bought a particular item (e.g., baby formula), also bought diapers" or other recommendations. They also play an important role in customer analytics, product clustering, catalog design, and store layout.

Dimensionality Reduction

This technique is used when the number of features or independent variables in a data set is too high. It reduces the number of data variables to a manageable size while preserving the data integrity. Dimensionality reduction is used in the preprocessing stage of data; when dealing with high dimensional data or data with a large number of features, it is often useful to reduce the dimensionality by projecting the data to a lower-dimensional subspace. The method should be used in a way so that it maintains the *essence* of the data. Many ML models use huge quantities of data with a number of features that may affect the accuracy of the models. This technique makes the models manageable. We discuss unsupervised learning algorithms in Chapter 7.

SemiSupervised Machine Learning Algorithms

These algorithms fall in between supervised and unsupervised learning. They are designed with both labeled and unlabeled data for training and may typically contain a small amount of labeled data and a large amount of unlabeled data. These systems may in some cases be more efficient and are able to considerably improve learning accuracy. The semisupervised learning methods are usually used when the labeled data requires skilled resources to train or learn from it. The acquired unlabeled data generally does not require additional resources.

- Semisupervised learning **falls in between supervised and unsupervised learning**. This method uses a small amount of labeled data and a large amount of unlabeled data to train a model. SSL works for a variety of problems from classification and regression to clustering and association.
- Since the method uses small amounts of labeled data and large amounts of unlabeled data, it reduces effort, time, and expense on manual annotation and reduces data preparation time.

Unsupervised and semisupervised learning can be more appealing alternatives as it can be time-consuming and costly to label data appropriately for supervised learning.

Reinforcement Learning (RL)

In this type of learning, the designed computer program interacts with a dynamic environment in which it has a specific goal to perform. This differs from standard supervised learning as no input/output pairs are provided, which involves finding a balance between exploration (of uncharted territory) and exploitation (of current knowledge).[6]. Examples of reinforced learning are playing a game against an opponent. In this type of learning, the computer program provides feedback in terms of rewards and punishments as it navigates its problem space.

RL is an ML **technique that trains the program to make decisions to achieve the most optimal results**. This method is based on rewarding desired behaviors and punishing undesired ones. RL is enforced through trial and error. It has applications in several disciplines including game theory, control theory, operations research, information theory, simulation-based optimization, multiagent systems, swarm intelligence, and statistics.

Some Fundamental Concepts Related to Machine Learning

Here, we discuss important terms and concepts used in building ML models.

HoldOut

In the **holdout** method, the largest data set is randomly divided into three subsets:

1. **A training set** is a subset of the data set that is used to build predictive models.
2. **The validation set** is a subset of the data set used to assess the performance of the model built in the training phase. This set allows for fine-tuning the parameters of the model and selecting the best-performing model. Validation may not be used for all types of models.
3. **Test sets are** the subset of the data used to assess the future performance of the model. If a model fits well to the training set but not as good to the test set, it is an indication of overfitting.

Cross Validation

The K-fold cross validation is used in case of the availability of a limited amount of data. The purpose is to obtain an unbiased estimation of the model performance.

Here, the data are divided into K subsets of equal sizes and the model fits K times leaving out one of the subsets from the training each time and using it as the test set.

If K equals the sample size, then this is called a *Leave-One-Out*.

Bootstrapping

- Bootstrapping is the technique used to make the estimations from the data by taking an average of the estimates from smaller data samples.
- The method involves iterative resampling of a data set with replacement.
- Resampling instead of only estimating the statistics once on complete data set, provides better results.
- Repeating this multiple times helps to obtain a vector of estimates.
- Bootstrapping calculates the variance, expected value, and other relevant statistics of these estimates.

Signal and Noise

- In ML, *signal* is the true underlying pattern that we wish to learn from the data.
- *Noise*, on the other hand, refers to irrelevant information or randomness in a data set.

The higher the noise, the lower the quality of the signal—and the signal-to-noise ratio—is. In ML, noise similarly refers to unwanted behaviors within the data that provide a low signal-to-noise ratio. Essentially, data = signal + noise.

One key difference between noise and signal is that a signal is intentional and carries meaningful information, while noise is unintentional and does not carry any information. In other words, a signal is created to transmit a specific message, while noise is an unwanted addition that can interfere with the message.

A signal, mathematically a function, is a mechanism for conveying information. Audio, image, electrocardiograph (ECG) signal, radar signals, stock price movements, electrical current/voltages, and so on are some of the examples.

A signal-to-noise ratio over 0 dB indicates that the signal level is greater than the noise level. The higher the ratio, the better the signal quality. For example, a Wi-Fi signal with S/N of 40 dB will deliver better network services than a signal with S/N of 20 dB.

Generally, a signal with an SNR value of 20 dB or more is recommended for data networks, whereas an SNR value of 25 dB or more is recommended for networks that use voice applications.

For example, an SNR of 95 dB, means that the level of the audio signal is 95 dB higher than the level of the noise. Which, in turn, means that an SNR of 95 dB is better than one that is 80 dB.

Signal is the desired information being transmitted, while noise is any unwanted or random interference that can affect the quality of the signal. A strong signal is essential to overcome any interference that may be present, and various techniques are used to minimize the impact of noise on the signal.

Goodness-of-Fit

The goodness-of-fit refers to how closely a model's prediction matches the observed (true) values.

Overfitting, Underfitting, and Bias-Variance Trade-Off

Underfitting refers to the case when a model is too simple or has a small number of features or regularized too much. These make the model inflexible in learning from the data set. *Underfitting* occurs when the model fails to capture important patterns in the training data set. Here the model is too simple or has too few explanatory variables.

This situation leads to high bias. The results show a systematic lack of fit in certain reasons.

Overfitting is the condition when the model performs well on the training set but poorly on the test set. The model is too flexible with too many features for training data. Flexibility allows to *memorize* the data including the noise. On the other hand, when the data contains too many features, trying to fit the predictors beyond a certain level might cause overfitting.

Bias and Variance

Bias and variance are two forms of prediction error in ML. Reducing errors from one might increase errors from the other. This trade-off between too simple (high bias) versus too complex (high variance) is a key concept in statistics and ML, and one that affects all supervised learning algorithms.

High variance means that the small changes in training data lead to big changes in the result. Variance is introduced with high sensitivity to variations in training data.

Bias is the type of error that occurs due to wrong assumptions about data. For example, assuming that the data are linear when it follows some other complex function.

Bias and variance are inversely related. It is impossible that an ML model has a low bias and a low variance. When the model is modified for a better fit, it leads to low bias but high variance.

How to Compute Bias and Variance?

- **Bias** is the distance from the average prediction and true value or the true value minus the mean (predictions).
- **Variance** is the average deviation from the average prediction or the mean (prediction minus mean (predictions)).
- **Bias and variance** help to optimize the error in our model and keep it as low as possible. An optimized model will be sensitive to the patterns in our data and will be able to generalize to new data.

In general, both the bias and variance should be low so as to prevent overfitting and underfitting.

Lazy Learners and Eager Learners

The lazy learner simply stores the training data and waits until testing data appears. Classification is done based on the most related data stored in training data. The K-NN algorithm is considered a lazy learner.

The other type of learner is known as **eager learners** that build a classification model based on the given training data before receiving data for classification. Because of the way the model is constructed, eager learners take a long time to train and less time to predict. Examples of this type of learner include decision trees, Naïve Bayes, and ANNs. Compared to eager learners, lazy learners take less training time and more prediction time. One example of the lazy learner is K-NN.

Summary

This chapter explores the field of ML, its importance, and the reasons behind the use of this field. ML is a method of designing systems that can learn, adjust, and improve based on the data fed to them without being explicitly programmed. ML applications are a way of analyzing and creating models from a very large sample or huge amounts of data commonly referred to as *big data*. ML can perform tasks without being explicitly programmed to do so. This chapter introduced ML as a subset of AI and explored this area including the definition, needs, and types of problems ML can solve.

An overview of ML along with the approach ML takes in solving problems is discussed. The broad categories of ML tasks are (1) supervised learning, (2) unsupervised learning, (3) semisupervised learning, and (4) reinforced learning along with the models used in supervised and unsupervised learning. The difference between supervised and unsupervised learning along with the models and algorithms used under both are explained briefly. The two major categories of supervised learning problems are regression and classification. Various types of regression models used are (1) OLSR, (2) linear regression/multiple regression, (3) logistic regression, (4) ridge regression, (5) nonlinear regression, (6) Lasso regression, and others were briefly discussed.

Classification is the other class of supervised learning. Different classification approaches and the models under classification are outlined in this chapter. The common classification tasks in ML are binary and multiclass classification. These along with the commonly used classification algorithms are discussed briefly. The following classification algorithms are discussed: logistic regression, Naïve Bayes, SVM, and K-nearest neighbors.

The chapter also introduced neural networks and deep learning. Neural networks and deep learning are the major application areas of ML. These were briefly introduced.

The other approaches to ML—semisupervised learning and RL—were also discussed.

Finally, the chapter discussed the metrics to evaluate the accuracy of classification and regression models and some important terms and concepts related to ML.

CHAPTER 3

Machine Learning Process, Associated Areas, and Managing Data in ML Models

Chapter Highlights

- Need and Justification for Using Machine Learning
- Machine Learning (ML) Process and Applications
- Machine Learning Problem-Solving Steps
- Machine Learning and Associated Areas
- Subsets of Machine Learning
- Machine Learning and Data Mining
- Other Associated Areas of Machine Learning
- A Brief Overview of Statistical Tools for Machine Learning
- General Statistical Skills
- Machine Learning (ML) and the Types and Role of Data in ML Process
- Data for ML Models and Managing Data Throughout the ML Process
  - Training Data Set
  - Validation Data Set
    - Hyperparameters
  - Test Data Set
- Determining the Size of Data Sets
- Machine Learning Problem-Solving Steps
- Summary

Need and Justification for the Use of Machine Learning Approach

A machine learning (ML) approach is used where no fully satisfactory algorithm is available. In cases where no definite solutions exist or vast numbers of potential answers exist, it is customary to label some of the correct answers as valid. To improve the algorithms(s) to achieve the best possible result, the algorithm is fed data commonly known as *training data* that the computer uses to improve the algorithm(s) to find correct answers. For example, to train a system for the task of digital character recognition, the MNIST data set of handwritten digits has often been used.[11]

ML works based on predictive and statistical algorithms that are provided to these machines. The algorithms are designed to learn and improve as more data flows through the system. Fraud detection, email spam, and GPS systems are some examples of ML applications.

ML applications are based on teaching a computer how to learn. Besides predictive and statistical algorithms, it also uses pattern recognition to draw conclusions from the data.

ML methods are used to develop complex models and algorithms that help to understand and make predictions or find patterns in the data. The analytical models in ML allow the analysts to make predictions by learning from the trends, patterns, and relationships in the historical data. ML automates model building. The algorithms in ML are designed to learn iteratively from data without being programmed.

According to Arthur Samuel, ML gives "computers the ability to learn without being explicitly programmed."[2][3] Samuel, an American pioneer in the field of *computer gaming* and artificial intelligence, coined the term *ML* in 1957 while at IBM.

ML algorithms are extensively used for data-driven decision making. Some other applications where ML has been used are email filtering, detection of network intruders or detecting a data breach, optical character recognition, learning to rank, computer vision, signal processing, and a wide range of engineering and business applications. ML is employed in a range of computing tasks. Most of these applications require huge amounts of data. ML makes it possible to handle and solve these types of problems. Often designing and programming explicit algorithms that are reproducible and have repeatability with good performance is difficult or infeasible.

Machine (ML) Process and Applications

In ML applications, huge amounts of data are needed, and it is challenging to develop programs to accomplish the task due to a large number of potential answers. One approach used in such cases is to label some correct answers as valid answers and use this as **training data**. Using the training data, the computer improves the algorithms to find the correct answer.

ML uses several approaches to teach computers to learn from huge amounts of high-quality data and focuses on prediction based on *known* properties learned from the *training data*.

ML models are built using training data. In regression models, the training set is a set of labeled examples $[x, f(x)]$ where x is the input variables and $f(x)$ is the label or observed target. The labels can be numerical or categorical. The goal of the ML algorithms is given a training set, find the approximation f of $f(x)$ that best generalizes or predicts labels for new examples. With high-quality data, ML can solve problems with high precision. Note that the algorithms are used to make predictions or draw conclusions without being explicitly

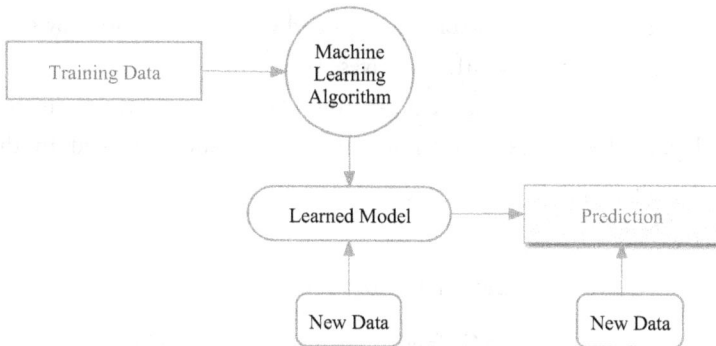

Figure 3.1 Process of achieving the end goal of prediction in machine learning

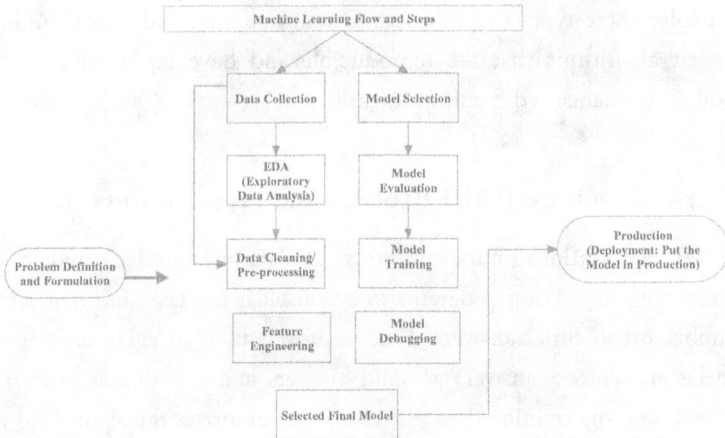

Figure 3.2 Machine learning workflow

programmed to do so.[2] Figure 3.1 shows how the training data and ML algorithms are used to achieve the end goal of making prediction.

The numerous applications of ML include engineering, business, and medical science. Some of the specific applications are cyber security, signal processing, wireless communications, email filtering, speech recognition, agriculture, and computer vision, to name a few. In these applications, it is usually difficult or unfeasible to develop conventional programs to perform the needed tasks.[3][4]

Machine Learning Problem-Solving Steps

Figure 3.2 outlines the overview of ML workflow. The flow in Figure 3.2 explains the ML problem-solving steps and approach. It also shows the role of data in achieving ML objectives.

Each of the steps in Figure 3.2—from Data collection to production (deploying the selected model in production)—are explained in the subsequent chapters.

Machine Learning and Associated Areas

Some of the key areas ML is associated with are as follows:

Data mining
Mathematical optimization
Computational statistics

These are considered subsets of ML. ML algorithms and models draw heavily from these areas. Computational statistics focus on making predictions using statistical methods and algorithms using computers but not all ML is statistical learning. The aim of *computational statistics* is implementing statistical methods on computers, [*sic*].[3]

The study of mathematical optimization delivers methods, theory, and application domains to the field of ML.

Data mining focuses on exploratory data analysis (EDA) through unsupervised learning.[6][7]

Subsets of Machine Learning (ML)

ML programs can perform tasks without being explicitly programmed. It involves computers learning from data fed to them to carry out specific tasks. For simple tasks assigned to computers, it is possible to program algorithms telling the machine how to execute all steps required to solve the problem at hand. In such cases, no learning on the part of computer is necessary.

For more advanced tasks, it can be challenging for a human to manually create the needed algorithms. In practice, it can turn out to be more effective to help the machine develop its own algorithm, rather than having human programmers specify every needed step.[11]

The discipline of ML employs various approaches to teach computers to accomplish tasks (find the best possible solutions). The associated areas of ML are shown in Figure 3.3. The figure shows the areas that have ties to ML. These are instrumental in arriving at ML problem solutions. Each of these areas are discussed in subsequent sections.

The associated areas are discussed in the following.

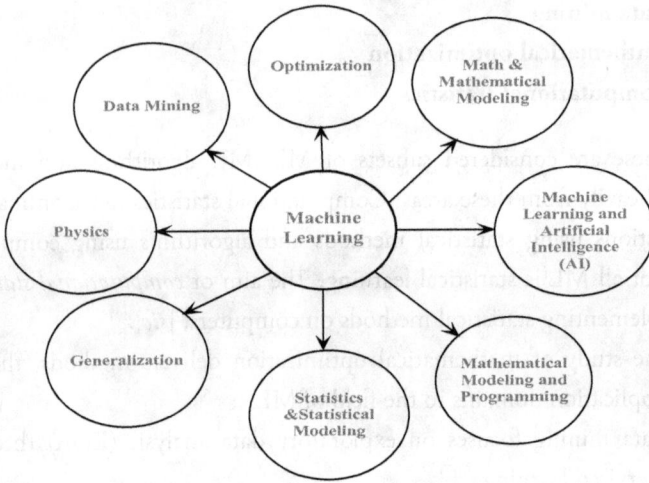

Figure 3.3 Machine learning and associated areas

Machine Learning and Data Mining

ML and data mining are similar in some ways and often overlap in applications. One of the tasks in ML is to make prediction based on *known* properties learned from the training data, whereas data mining algorithms are used for the discovery of (previously) *unknown* patterns. Data mining is concerned with Knowledge Discovery in Databases (or KDD).

Data mining uses many ML methods. On the other hand, ML also employs data mining methods as *unsupervised learning* or as a preprocessing step to improve learner accuracy. The goals are somewhat different. The performance of ML is usually evaluated with respect to the ability to *reproduce known* knowledge. In data mining, which is knowledge discovery from the data (KDD), the key task is the discovery of previously *unknown* knowledge. Unlike ML which is evaluated with respect to known knowledge, data mining uses uninformed or unsupervised methods that often outperform compared to other supervised methods. In a typical KDD task, supervised methods cannot be used due to the unavailability of training data. Figure 3.4 outlines the predictive and descriptive data mining learning techniques along with supervised and unsupervised learning techniques.

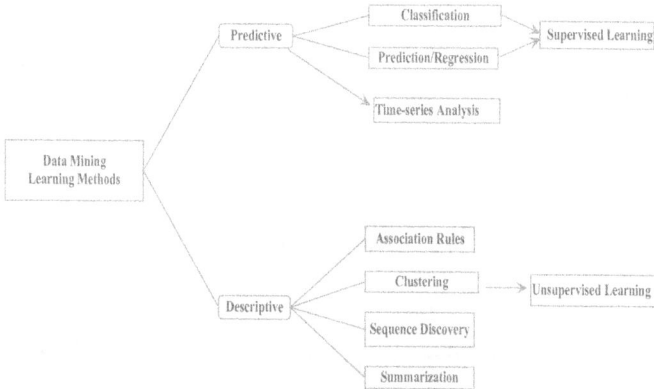

Figure 3.4 Predictive and descriptive data mining

Several data mining and ML methods overlap in applications. As indicated earlier, data mining is concerned with knowledge discovery from the data (KDD) where the key task is the discovery of previously *unknown* knowledge. ML, on the other hand, is evaluated with respect to known knowledge.[13][14][15][16]

ML methods use complex models and algorithms that allow the analysts to make predictions by learning from the trends, patterns, and relationships in the historical data. The algorithms are designed to learn iteratively from data without being programmed. In a way, ML automates model building.

Machine-learning algorithms have extensive applications in data-driven predictions and are a major decision-making tool. Some applications where ML has been used are email filtering, cyber security, signal processing, fraud detection, and others. ML is employed in a range of computing tasks. Although machine-learning models are being used in several applications, it has limitations in designing and programming explicit algorithms that are reproducible and have repeatability with good performance. With current research and the use of newer technology, the fields of ML and artificial intelligence are becoming more promising.

It is important to note that data mining uses unsupervised methods that usually outperform the supervised methods used in ML. Data mining is the application of knowledge discovery from data where supervised methods cannot be used due to the unavailability of training data. ML may also employ data mining methods such as *unsupervised learning* to improve learner accuracy. The performance of ML algorithms depends on their ability to *reproduce known knowledge.*

Other Associated Areas of Machine Learning

Optimization

In many applications, the ML problems are formulated to minimize some loss function where the goal is the minimization of some loss function on a training set of data. Loss functions indicate the difference or the discrepancy between the predictions of the model being trained and the actual problem instances. For example, in classification problems, a label is assigned to the instances and models are trained to correctly predict the preassigned labels of a set of examples.[33][16]

Generalization

In ML, generalization is the ability of the model to adapt to new data that is usually drawn from the unknown probability distribution or from the same distribution as the one used to create and train the model. Thus, generalization is how accurately the learning machine performs on new previously unseen data or examples. It is about creating a general model that can produce accurate predictions in new cases.

Generalization of learning algorithms is an active topic of research in machine and **deep learning**.

Physics

Analytical and computational techniques of statistical physics have been applied in ML. Statistical physics has been applied in medical diagnostics.[37]

Other ML tools including variation inference and maximum entropy are derived from statistical physics. Although statistical physics is not a prerequisite for ML and AI, a background in physics is helpful.

Statistics

Statistics is a major component of ML and data analytics. Statistics and ML are closely related fields. Statistics and statistical tools are widely used in ML. Both descriptive and inferential statistics tools are applied to visualize data to extract unseen patterns and draw inference. The broader analytics tools including the descriptive, predictive, and prescriptive analytics have applications in ML. A career in ML requires a deep understanding of statistics and programming. The popular computer software to apply statistical concepts and programming are R-statistical programming language and Python. The overall field of ML and statistics is termed data science that we discussed in Chapter 1. The term data science was suggested by Michael I. Jordan,

We have briefly presented the tools and techniques of statistics below—the knowledge of which is essential in learning ML and its applications.

For statistical applications, Leo Breiman suggested two types of statistical modeling: data model and algorithmic model.[29] The *algorithmic model* means more or less the ML algorithms like random forest.

A Brief Overview of Statistical Tools for Machine Learning

Businesses generate and consume massive amounts of data and rely on data for decision making. The data must be processed and analyzed using appropriate tools. Statistics is about making sense of data. Data scientists are usually not formally trained in statistics. Since statistics is at the core of ML, ML professionals should be trained in statistics and data analysis to properly understand, analyze, and interpret statistical models. Statistics and data analysis constitute the tools and methods that help understand, analyze, and interpret results.

Statistics is divided into two broad categories—descriptive statistics and inferential statistics.

Descriptive statistics are about describing data. It uses charts and graphs or visual tools and numerical methods. Graphical methods are very effective in visualizing the patterns in the data and using these patterns to describing distributions. Probability distributions are powerful tools in making decisions from the data. Recently, several application software like Tableau is widely used to visualize patterns in big data.

Inferential statistics tools are used to draw conclusions from sample data. It is the process of drawing conclusion about the population using the sample data. In statistics, we almost always rely on the sample data to draw conclusions about the population as in many cases, the population from which the samples are drawn is huge and it is not usually possible to study the entire population.

Statistics studies variation. Almost all data show variation and statistics is the tool that studies variation in the data. The two main reasons for studying statistics are: (1) statistics allows us to study variation and (2) the tools of statistics are used to draw conclusion using limited data.

Statistics and ML are two closely related areas of study. ML uses huge amounts of data and statistical tools and models to solve problems. It is usually not possible to solve real-world problems with ML without a good understanding of statistical fundamentals.

The major tools of statistics used to solve ML problems include EDA, probability and probability distributions, sampling and estimation theory, hypothesis testing, design of experiment (DOE) models, and others. These tools play an integral role in solving problems across many ML applications.

The other major tools used in solving ML problems are regression and classification methods. The regression models—from simple regression, multiple regressions, ridge regression to many other types of regression—are widely used. These methods are used in training ML data depending on the applications.

General Statistics Skills

Here is a summary of the general statistical skills required for ML.

- Define problems that are sound and statistically answerable.
- Calculate and interpret simple statistical tools including descriptive statistics, EDA tools, EDA, and data visualization techniques to explain and communicate the findings.
- Understand mathematical statistical tools and their applications.
- Under the concepts behind the central limit theorem and the law of large numbers.
- Apply the major inferential statistics tools including the sampling theory, estimation, hypothesis testing, and analysis of variance (ANOVA).
- Be able to establish relationships between the target variable and the independent variables or the features using appropriate statistical models.
- Design statistical hypothesis testing experiments, A/B testing, and so on, and design experiments using DOE techniques.
- Be able to understand and interpret various regression and classification models.
- Be able to calculate and interpret performance metrics, for example, p-value, alpha, type I and type II errors, power of tests.

Machine Learning (ML) Process and the Types of Data in ML Process

ML process heavily depends on data and data are key to ML. Managing and using data is critical to ML.

ML solutions are as good as the data and the ML process heavily depends on the quality of data. It is important to learn how to use and manage data throughout the ML process.

One of the major goals of ML is to construct or design algorithms that are used to make and improve predictions by learning from large quantities of data. ML models are effective when high-quality data are used. Thus, ML is a data-driven decision-making process where the predictions are made using **mathematical models** from the input data. The input data used to build the models are divided into three data sets and are used in different stages of the model creation and testing.

Data for ML Models and Managing Data Throughout ML Process

In the ML model-building process, the data are divided or partitioned into three categories and are used in different phases of model building. The data sets are as follows:

- **Training data set**
- **Validation data**
- **Test data**

Training Data Set

The training data set is a set on which the model is fit initially. The training data set consists of pairs of input and output vectors (or scalers). The inputs are often termed as independent variables or *attributes* or *features* and the output or the answer key is termed as *label*, or *target*, or dependent (response) variable.

The training data is a set of examples used to fit the **parameters** of the models. These parameters may be the weights of connectors between the neurons in **artificial neural networks** or a **classifi**er or a **Naïve Bays classifier** that are trained using the training data set using a *supervised learning* method or using optimization methods (e.g., *gradient descent*).

Parameters are internal to the model and are learned or estimated purely from the data during the training as the algorithm used tries to learn the mapping between the input features and the labels or targets.

In the initial phase of the training, parameters are initialized to some values (random values or set to zeros). The initial values are updated as the training progresses using an optimization algorithm like gradient descent. The learning algorithm continuously updates the parameter values in the learning process. At the end of training or learning, the updated parameters are the model parameters. Some examples of parameters are the coefficients of the regression modes (linear, multiple, or logistics regression models), weights in the neural networks, or the centroid of the clusters in clustering algorithms.

In ML and deep learning, the parameters are the values the learning algorithm can change independently during the learning process. It is important to note that the parameter values are affected by the choice of *hyperparameters* set before training begins and the learning algorithm uses them to learn the parameters.

As indicated, the parameters are internal to the model and are learned or estimated purely from the data during the training. These parameters are continuously updated, and the final parameters are the parameters at the end of the training process. The hyperparameters are set before the training process. Setting the right hyperparameter values is critical as it directly affects the model's performance. The process of setting the hyperparameters is called hyperparameter tuning.

The initial model is run using the training data set. The result produced by the model is compared with the target for each input vector in the training set. Based on the result of the comparison and the type of learning algorithm used, the model parameters are adjusted. The model fitting is an iterative process and involves both *variable selection* and *parameter estimation* (https://towardsdatascience.com/parameters-and-hyperparameters-aa609601a9ac).

Validation Data Set[3]

In the second phase, the model fitted in the first stage using the training data is used to predict the responses using another set of observations known as the **validation data set**. This new data set known as the validation set provides an unbiased evaluation of the model fit used by the training set by tuning the *hyperparameters*.

Hyperparameters

Hyperparameters are parameters whose values control the learning process and determine the values of model parameters that a learning algorithm ends up learning. The prefix *hyper_* suggests that they are *top-level* parameters that control the learning process and the model parameters that result from it.

In ML models, the hyperparameter values are set by the ML engineer usually before the model training begins. These parameters are external to the model and the model cannot change these values during the model training or learning.

Hyperparameters are used by the model in the model training process, but these are not the part of the resulting model that results at the end of the training process. At the end of the learning, we have the trained model. It is usually not known what hyperparameter values were used to train the model, we only know the trained model parameter values.

It is important to note that hyperparameters are values we decide before the model training begins and they remain the same at the end of the training. Some examples include number of hidden layers in neural networks, number of iterations in training a neural network, number of clusters in a clustering algorithm, learning rate in optimization algorithms (e.g., gradient descent), the cost function or loss function the model will use, and others.

It is important to understand the difference between hyperparameters and parameters. The hyperparameters affect the parameters the model learns but the hyperparameters are unchanged.

The difference between the test and validation data set is that the training data set is a set of data used to fit the model. A validation data set is a subset of data used to provide an objective assessment of a model's fit on the training data while changing hyperparameters.

Test Data Set

The test data set is a subset of the training data set that is utilized to give an objective evaluation of a final model. It is a set of examples used to assess the performance or generalization of a fully specified classifier.[8][9] A test data set is independent of the training data. It should follow the same probability distribution as the training data set. If the model fits well to the training set and also fits the test data set, it is an indication of minimal **overfitting**.

Overfitting occurs when the model provides accurate predictions for the training data but not for new data. The reasons for overfitting are (i) the training data has too much noise, (ii) the model being fitted is too complex and learns the noise in the training data set, and (iii) the training data set is too small. One of the methods of testing for overfitting is **K-fold cross-validation**.

Underfitting is another undesirable condition in models. This occurs when the model cannot establish a meaningful relationship between the input and output data. Underfit models provide inaccurate results for both the training and test data sets, and they have a high bias. Overfit models have high variance. Overfit models provide accurate results for the training data set but not for the test set. In model training, it is important to find a trade-off between bias and variance.

Determining the Size of Data Sets

Dividing the data set accurately is critical to creating a successful and effective ML model. Dividing the data set in training, validation, and test sets is about determining the size of each set. While more training data should lead to a more accurate model, a smaller amount of test and validation data may provide a more biased estimate of the model and its performance. So, there is a need for a balance between these sets. If a large quantity of data is available, a 60-20-20 split is suggested in the literature. There is also an 80-10-10 split used. When the data set is small. A smaller test may not provide a good enough representation, so in practice, a K-fold cross-validation may be used. Suggestions regarding splitting of the data sets into training, validation, and test sets can be found in the references below.

1. https://glassboxmedicine.com/2019/09/15/best-use-of-train-val-test-splits-with-tips-for-medical-data/#:~:text=Common%20rat ios%20used%20are%3A,20%25 %20val%2C%2020%25 %20test.

2. https://deepchecks.com/training-validation-and-test-sets-what-are-the-differences/.

In machine learning algorithm, we split the data set in a certain ratio training, validation, and test data set. The model is built on a training data set. The test data set is used for the evaluation of the model efficiency.

Machine Learning Problem-Solving Steps

Almost every ML project goes through the following steps. These are:

1. **Defining the problem and the problem statement:** this is usually the first step in an ML project. The tools used in this step are EDA and data mining.
2. **Data exploration:** the major statistical tools used in this step are descriptive statistics, EDA, and data visualization tools.
3. **Data preparation and data cleaning:** these involve dealing with missing values, dealing with data corruption and data errors (from a bad sensor), and unformatted data (observations with different scales). Some of the cleaning methods include the knowledge of outlier detection and missing value imputation.
4. **Data preparation, transformation, and standardization**
   o If data have errors and contain inconsistencies, it cannot be used in training the ML models. In such cases, the techniques used are data transformation and standardization of the data. The data might need to go through a set of transformations to change its shape or structure that makes it more suitable for the algorithms being used.
   o The techniques used in this case are data **sampling, feature selection methods, data transformation, scaling, encoding,** and **standardization.**
5. **Model selection and evaluation**
   o A key step in solving a predictive analytics problem in ML is selecting and evaluating the appropriate model and learning method. There are several statistical models and modeling techniques used to approach these problems.

Some of the statistical tools that are helpful in the process are **experimental design and DOE.** Experimental design is a part of statistics that is very useful in the initial stage of the model. It is also used in the feature selection and evaluation process of a model. The other tools used in conjunction with DOE are **statistical hypothesis testing** and **estimation theory**. The use of all these tools requires a good foundation and understanding of statistics.

Fine-Tuning the Model

Almost all ML algorithms use hyperparameters that are used to customize the training and refine the models.

The values of hyperparameters **control the learning process and help determine the values of model parameters that a learning or training algorithm uses as improved model**. The *hyper_* means that these are *top-level* parameters that control the learning process and establish the final model parameters that are used by the model.

Some of the examples of hyperparameters are **the number of nodes and the layers in a neural network or the number of branches in a decision tree**. Hyperparameters also determine the model architecture, learning rate, and model complexity.

A model starts the training process with random parameter values and adjusts them throughout, whereas hyperparameters are **outside of the model and are set by the analyst before the model training**. The values of hyperparameters are expected to improve the model accuracy but it is not always the case. They may have adverse effects on the model. The hyperparameter tuning is empirical in nature and requires many experiments to evaluate the effect of different hyperparameter settings on the performance of the model. Figure 3.5 outlines the above steps.

Summary

This chapter discusses the ML process, associated areas of ML, data used, and the way the data are divided and managed in building ML models. The major topics of discussion include the need and justification for using ML, ML applications, ML problem-solving steps, associated areas, and subsets of ML.

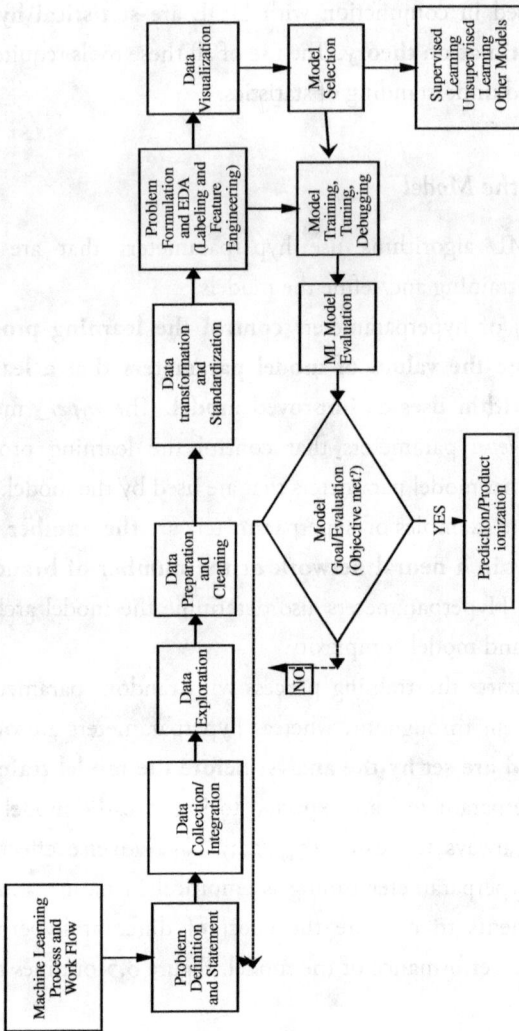

Figure 3.5 Steps in solving a machine learning problem

Some of the subsets or the areas ML interacts with to solve the problems include computational statistics, mathematical optimization, data mining, statistics, and programming. These areas are explained briefly.

ML uses huge amounts of data and statistical tools and models to solve problems. It is usually not possible to solve real-world ML problems without a good understanding of statistics.

The major tools of statistics used to solve ML problems include EDA, probability and probability distributions, sampling and estimation theory, hypothesis testing, DOE, and others. These tools play an integral role in solving problems across all ML applications.

ML heavily depends on data and data are key to building ML models. Managing and using data is critical to ML. ML solutions are as good as the data. The ML process heavily depends on the quality of data. It is important to learn how to use and manage data throughout the ML process. The chapter discusses the way the data are divided and managed throughout the ML process.

ML is a data-driven decision-making process where the decisions are made using *models*. The input data used to build the models are divided into three data sets and are used in different stages of the model creation and testing. The three categories are training data set, validation data set, and test data. Each of these sets, the recommended size and proportion of these sets are discussed.

Finally, this chapter discusses the steps in solving ML problems. Every ML problem goes through these steps—problem definition and problem statement, data exploration, data preparation and data cleaning, data transformation and standardization, model selection and evaluation, and fine-tuning the model. These steps and the role of statistics in these steps are discussed. The chapter also provided an overview of statistical tools in ML.

PART 3

Machine Learning Models

CHAPTER 4

Libraries and Algorithms Used in Machine Learning, Data, and ML Models

Chapter Highlights

- Prerequisites, Libraries, and Algorithms Used in Machine Learning
- Packages to Solve Machine Learning Problems
- Packages Described Briefly
- Accessing and Using the Packages
- Summary

Introduction: Prerequisites

The purpose of this book is to introduce machine learning to students and professionals interested in data science and machine learning and to those who are planning to dig deeper by taking other courses in this field. The book is also suitable for managers, technical professionals, and product and process engineers and managers.

Since machine learning is applied mathematics, knowledge of different areas of statistics, linear algebra, and programming is very helpful. Among different areas of statistics, one needs to understand *descriptive statistics* including data and different types of data, manipulating data using grouping and frequency distribution, basic concepts of probability, probability distributions (both discrete and continuous), a thorough understanding of normal or Gaussian distribution, numerical measures of data, such as central tendency, percentiles, and the concepts of variance and standard deviation. Besides these, the understanding of covariance and correlation that provide the numerical measure of the relationship among the variables is very helpful. The other important tools often applied are data visualization or graphical tools, and exploratory data analysis (EDA) techniques. These statistical concepts are used to evaluate the accuracy of machine learning models. All these areas come under *descriptive statistics*.

Besides the knowledge of descriptive statistics, a knowledge of *inferential statistics* or inference procedures is also needed to understand and apply the machine learning models. Inferential statistics is the process of drawing conclusions from sample data about the population from which data are gathered. This is the process of generalization where we rely on the sample data to draw inference about the population. In machine learning, huge amounts of data are used to build models. These are often samples.

Many of the machine learning models are inference procedures. Among these are classification, regression, analysis of variance, clustering, decision trees, and many other models in regression and classification. These are discussed in detail in Chapter 6—dedicated to supervised and unsupervised learning.

The other important machine learning models are neural networks. Neural networks are designed to work with huge quantities of data at a very large scale. Neural networks or artificial neural networks (ANN) are computational systems that *learn* to perform tasks by considering examples, generally without being programmed with any task-specific rules.

One of the most important applications of machine learning is deep learning.

Libraries and Algorithms Used in Machine Learning

Machine learning is the practice of teaching a computer to learn. The concept uses pattern recognition, as well as other forms of predictive algorithms, to make judgments on incoming data. This field is closely related to artificial intelligence and computational statistics.

Machine learning draws from various fields including mathematics, statistics, computer science, and programming. The field uses a number of technologies and computer applications. In recent years, there has been a trend to automate the machine learning process. The following is a partial list of technologies (software and libraries) used in solving data science and machine learning problems. Note that the technologies are derived from different fields including statistics, data visualization, programming, machine learning, and big data.

Python has become a popular language for data science. There has been increasing demand for it. Some examples are provided to introduce the readers to Python. These examples also provide steps to get started with this software. To be able to run Python and its libraries, the first step is to install Python 3 (it is the most recent version of Python). Python can be run using Jupyter Notebook which is a Python interface. Python and Python libraries are usually implemented using ***Anaconda Distribution***.

There are other ways to download and install Python 3. One way is to follow the instructions at anaconda.com. The other way to get to Jupyter Notebook is by using Google's Colaboratory service: colab.research.google.com/.

Anaconda Distribution is free, easy to install, and offers free community support. The details of Anaconda Distribution and installation can be found in:

https://docs.anaconda.com/free/anaconda/getting-started/what-is-distro/

Anaconda Distribution is a free Python/R data science distribution that contains:

- conda—a package and environment manager for your command line interface.
- Anaconda Navigator—a desktop application built on conda, with options to launch other development applications from your managed environments.
- Two hundred and fifty automatically installed packages that work well together out of the box.
- Access to the Anaconda Public Repository, with 8000 open-source data science and machine learning packages.

Some of the widely used Python libraries and applications are described here.

Jupyter Notebook

Jupyter Notebook is an interactive web interface for Python that is used in machine learning applications of data science. One way of implementing and using Python programming language and its libraries is through Jupyter Notebook. To open the Jupyter Notebook:

1. Open Anaconda, then click Anaconda (Navigator).
2. In Anaconda.Navigator, click launch CMD.Exe Prompt.
3. In the Command prompt (cmd.exe) screen, type, **Jupyter Notebook.**

This should open a new notebook. All the activities in the chapters will be developed using Jupyter Notebook. It is suggested that for each exercise you open a new Jupyter Notebook and save it with an appropriate name so that you can identify those notebooks easily. In the exercises in subsequent sections, you will be asked to open a Jupyter Notebook.

The **Jupyter Notebook** is a language-agnostic HTML notebook application for Project Jupyter. Jupyter Notebooks are documents that allow for creating and sharing live code, equations, visualizations, and narrative text together. These are used for data cleaning and transformation, numerical simulation, statistical modeling, data visualization, machine learning, and much more.

Python

Python is a programming language designed by Guido van Rossum. Python was designed to be easily read by programmers. Because of its large libraries, Python can be implemented and used to do anything from web pages to scientific research.

Python has a simple syntax that is commonly used for data science.[35] As noted earlier, Python is the most widely used programming language in machine learning. To follow the machine learning applications, the following libraries are used—NumPy, pandas, Matplotlib, scikit-learn, and others. This is a partial list. Important libraries are explained.

Scikit-Learn

Scikit-learn is a widely used Python module for machine learning. It is built on top of SciPy. Among the several Python libraries which provide solid implementations of a range of machine learning algorithms, **Scikit-Learn** is the best-known package that provides efficient versions of a large number of common algorithms. Scikit-Learn is characterized by a clean, uniform, and streamlined application programming interface (API), as well as by very useful and complete online documentation. A benefit of this uniformity is that once you understand the basic use and syntax of Scikit-Learn for one type of model, switching to a new model or algorithm is very straightforward.

TensorFlow is an open-source library that was created by Google. It is used to design, build, and train deep learning models. TensorFlow is considered difficult to both learn and use for beginners, because of the programming skill needed.

Pandas

Pandas is a flexible and powerful data analysis/manipulation library for Python, providing labeled data structures like R data frame objects, statistical functions, and much more. Pandas is a machine learning tool used for data cleaning and analysis. It is used for exploring, cleaning, transforming preparing data for visualizing. Pandas is an open-source Python package built on top of NumPy. It is used as one of the most important data cleaning and analysis tools. It provides fast, flexible, and expressive data structures. To install pandas in Jupyter Notebook use this command:

! pip install pandas

To import pandas in Jupyter Notebook, use:

import pandas as pd

Note: If you install Jupyter Notebook, Pandas and many other application packages are installed automatically.

Visualization With Matplotlib

Matplotlib is a package for visualization in Python. Matplotlib is a multiplatform data visualization library built on NumPy arrays and designed to work with the broader SciPy stack. It was conceived by John Hunter in 2002, originally as a patch to IPython for enabling interactive MATLAB-style plotting. It is a powerful graphing/charting tool that works with Pandas and NumPy.

NumPy

NumPy (short for *Numerical Python*) provides an efficient interface to store and operate on dense data buffers. This tool is used to work with very large matrices. In some ways, NumPy arrays are like Python's built-in list type, but NumPy arrays provide much more efficient storage and data operations as the arrays grow larger in size. NumPy arrays form the core of nearly the entire ecosystem of data science tools in Python, so time spent learning to use NumPy effectively will be valuable no matter what aspect of data science interests you.

To install NumPy in Jupyter Notebook use this command:

!pip install numpy`

To import numpy as np in Jupyter Notebook, use:

import numpy as np

Seaborn

Python Seaborn library is a widely used package for data visualization that sits on top of Matplotlib and is built on top of the matplotlib data visualization library. It can also perform EDA. Seaborn is used to explore and understand data. The plotting functions in Seaborn operate on data frames and arrays containing whole data sets. It utilizes simple sets of techniques to produce images in Python. Matplotlib, on the other hand, is highly customized and robust.

In order to install the Seaborn library in Python, you can use **! pip install seaborn or** import it in Jupyter notebook.

Some Other Technologies Used in Machine Learning

- R statistical analysis is a programming language that was designed for statistics and data mining[36] applications and is one of the popular application packages used by data scientists and analysts.
- PyTorch is another framework for machine learning developed by Facebook.
- Tableau makes a variety of software that is used for data visualization.[37] It is a widely used software for big data applications and is used for descriptive analytics and data visualization.
- Apache Hadoop is a software framework that is used to process data over large distributed systems.
- Automating the machine learning problem: SAS machine learning, Microsoft Auto Machine Learning: Azur.

Summary

This chapter briefly discussed the prerequisites for machine learning. Machine learning draws from different areas including mathematics, computer science programming, and others. A background in Statistics and statistical modeling, linear algebra, and programming language, for example, Python, is a widely used programming language used in machine learning. The chapter provided instructions on downloading Python 3 and running the program using Jupyter Notebook. Python and Python libraries are usually implemented using **Anaconda Distribution**. The details of Anaconda Distribution and installation steps are provided. The chapter also discussed some of the commonly used libraries in machine learning and described these packages briefly. Some instructions on accessing and using these packages are also described.

Machine Learning (ML) Libraries, Data Representation, Problem Formulation, and EDA

PART 2

Machine Learning (ML) Libraries, Data Representation, Problem Formulation, and EDA

CHAPTER 5

Working With Data

Chapter Highlights

- Loading and Working With Data
  Data Representation (Data Samples, Features,
  Dimensionality, Matrix Representation)
- Data Visualization and EDA (Histograms, Time Series,
  Images)
- Data Preprocessing (Normalization, Standardization,
  Dimensionality Reduction Techniques)
- Summary

Loading a Data Set and creating Feature and Target Matrices

Loading a data set for machine learning applications is usually done using Python and implemented using *Jupyter Notebook*. We will demonstrate here the steps for loading a data set and creating features and target matrices. Machine learning models are created using data. Therefore, the first step is to load the data in a format that the program understands.

One of the ways of loading data for analysis is using *seaborn*, which is a Python library. The data are represented as a table or matrix. Most data tables for machine learning applications are two-dimensional containing rows and columns. Each row represents one observation commonly known as an *instance*, and each column represents an independent variable or a *feature*.

Importing Data Using Python and Seaborn in Jupyter Notebook

If you are using Anaconda, open Anaconda navigation and follow the instructions below:

1. **Open Jupyter Notebook and type the codes below to import Seaborn**
   import seaborn as sns
2. **Check the version of sns, type**
   sns. __version__
   '0.11.0'
3. **Check how many available data sets are in Seaborn, type**
   sns.get_dataset_names ()

The preloaded data sets in the Seaborn library list will be displayed as shown below. These are available to the users. You can also upload your data set. Uploading data set using .cvs file is explained later.

['anagrams',
'anscombe',
'attention',
'Brain_networks',
'Car_crashes',
'diamonds',
'dots',
'dowjones',
'exercise',
'flights',
'fmri',
'geyser',
'glue',
'healthexp',
'iris',
'mpg',
'penguins',
'planets',

'seaice',

'taxis',

'tips',

'titanic']

4. **Call a data set and check whether it has been loaded (here we are loading the 'diamonds' data set from the preloaded data sets and print the first five instances)**

df=sns. load_dataset('diamonds')

df. head ()

	carat	cut	color	clarity	depth	table	price	x	y	z
0	0.23	Ideal	E	SI2	61.5	55.0	326	3.95	3.98	2.43
1	0.21	Premium	E	SI1	59.8	61.0	326	3.89	3.84	2.31
2	0.23	Good	E	VS1	56.9	65.0	327	4.05	4.07	2.31
3	0.29	Premium	I	VS2	62.4	58.0	334	4.20	4.23	2.63
4	0.31	Good	J	SI2	63.3	58.0	335	4.34	4.35	2.75

5. **Load another data set**

df=sns. load_dataset('iris')

df. head ()

	sepal_length	sepal_width	petal_length	petal_width	species
0	5.1	3.5	1.4	0.2	setosa
1	4.9	3.0	1.4	0.2	setosa
2	4.7	3.2	1.3	0.2	setosa
3	4.6	3.1	1.5	0.2	setosa
4	5.0	3.6	1.4	0.2	setosa

6. **To see the last five entries**

df. tail ()

	sepal_length	sepal_width	petal_length	petal_width	species
145	6.7	3.0	5.2	2.3	virginica
146	6.3	2.5	5.0	1.9	virginica
147	6.5	3.0	5.2	2.0	virginica
148	6.2	3.4	5.4	2.3	virginica
149	5.9	3.0	5.1	1.8	virginica

7. **To check the shape of the data (rows and columns)**
df. shape
(150, 5)

8. **Loading another data set called *tips* and checking the shape**
data=sns. load_dataset('tips')
data. head (15)

	total_bill	tip	sex	smoker	day	time	size
0	16.99	1.01	Female	No	Sun	Dinner	2
1	10.34	1.66	Male	No	Sun	Dinner	3
2	21.01	3.50	Male	No	Sun	Dinner	3
3	23.68	3.31	Male	No	Sun	Dinner	2
4	24.59	3.61	Female	No	Sun	Dinner	4
5	25.29	4.71	Male	No	Sun	Dinner	4
6	8.77	2.00	Male	No	Sun	Dinner	2
7	26.88	3.12	Male	No	Sun	Dinner	4
8	15.04	1.96	Male	No	Sun	Dinner	2
9	14.78	3.23	Male	No	Sun	Dinner	2
10	10.27	1.71	Male	No	Sun	Dinner	2
11	35.26	5.00	Female	No	Sun	Dinner	4
12	15.42	1.57	Male	No	Sun	Dinner	2
13	18.43	3.00	Male	No	Sun	Dinner	4
14	14.83	3.02	Female	No	Sun	Dinner	2

data. shape
(244, 7)

The above examples illustrate the steps for importing data for analysis. The next few steps will demonstrate how to create features and target matrices.

Importing Data Using Seaborn Into a Jupyter Notebook and Creating Feature and Target Matrices

1. **Open a Jupyter Notebook.**
import seaborn as sns

2. **Load the *diamonds* data set and print the first 10 instances.**
diamonds=sns. load_dataset ('diamonds')
diamonds. head (10)

	carat	cut	color	clarity	depth	table	price	x	y	z
0	0.23	Ideal	E	SI2	61.5	55.0	326	3.95	3.98	2.43
1	0.21	Premium	E	SI1	59.8	61.0	326	3.89	3.84	2.31
2	0.23	Good	E	VS1	56.9	65.0	327	4.05	4.07	2.31
3	0.29	Premium	I	VS2	62.4	58.0	334	4.20	4.23	2.63
4	0.31	Good	J	SI2	63.3	58.0	335	4.34	4.35	2.75
5	0.24	Very Good	J	VVS2	62.8	57.0	336	3.94	3.96	2.48
6	0.24	Very Good	I	VVS1	62.3	57.0	336	3.95	3.98	2.47
7	0.26	Very Good	H	SI1	61.9	55.0	337	4.07	4.11	2.53
8	0.22	Fair	E	VS2	65.1	61.0	337	3.87	3.78	2.49
9	0.23	Very Good	H	VS1	59.4	61.0	338	4.00	4.05	2.39

3. **Check the shape of the *diamonds* data set (rows and columns).**

diamonds. shape

(53940, 10)

The diamond data set has 53,940 instances (rows) and 10 columns or features. We select ***price*** as the target as it seems logical to predict the price using the other features.

We create a variable X to store the features and a variable Y to store the target matrix and use indexing to access only the values from the column *price*.

4. **Create a variable X to store the features by using drop (). The drop () function will include all of the features except the target *price*. Also, print the first 10 instances.**

X=diamonds.drop('price', axis=1)

X.head (10)

	carat	cut	color	clarity	depth	table	x	y	z
0	0.23	Ideal	E	SI2	61.5	55.0	3.95	3.98	2.43
1	0.21	Premium	E	SI1	59.8	61.0	3.89	3.84	2.31
2	0.23	Good	E	VS1	56.9	65.0	4.05	4.07	2.31
3	0.29	Premium	I	VS2	62.4	58.0	4.20	4.23	2.63
4	0.31	Good	J	SI2	63.3	58.0	4.34	4.35	2.75
5	0.24	Very Good	J	VVS2	62.8	57.0	3.94	3.96	2.48

(Continued)

	carat	cut	color	clarity	depth	table	x	y	z
6	0.24	Very Good	I	VVS1	62.3	57.0	3.95	3.98	2.47
7	0.26	Very Good	H	SI1	61.9	55.0	4.07	4.11	2.53
8	0.22	Fair	E	VS2	65.1	61.0	3.87	3.78	2.49
9	0.23	Very Good	H	VS1	59.4	61.0	4.00	4.05	2.39

5. **Create a variable Y to store the target matrix by using drop ().**
   Print the first 10 instances.

   Y=diamonds['price']

   Y. head (10)

   0 326

   1 326

   2 327

   3 334

   4 335

   5 336

   6 336

   7 337

   8 337

   9 338

   Name: price, dtype: int64

6. **Print out the shape of variables X and Y.**

   X.shape

   (53940, 9)

   Y. shape

   (53940,)

Reading CSV File Into a Jupyter Notebook Using Pandas and Creating Feature and Target Matrices.

```
import pandas as pd
df=pd. read_csv ("C:\\Users\\asahay\\OneDrive \Documents\\
Diamonds.csv")
df.head()
```

	Column_1	carat	cut	color	clarity	depth	table	price	x	y	z
0	1	0.23	Ideal	E	SI2	61.5	55.0	326	3.95	3.98	2.43
1	2	0.21	Premium	E	SI1	59.8	61.0	326	3.89	3.84	2.31
2	3	0.23	Good	E	VS1	56.9	65.0	327	4.05	4.07	2.31
3	4	0.29	Premium	I	VS2	62.4	58.0	334	4.20	4.23	2.63
4	5	0.31	Good	J	SI2	63.3	58.0	335	4.34	4.35	2.75

df.tail()

	Column_1	carat	cut	color	clarity	depth	table	price	x	y	z
53935	53936	0.72	Ideal	D	SI1	60.8	57.0	2757	5.75	5.76	3.50
53936	53937	0.72	Good	D	SI1	63.1	55.0	2757	5.69	5.75	3.61
53937	53938	0.70	Very Good	D	SI1	62.8	60.0	2757	5.66	5.68	3.56
53938	53939	0.86	Premium	H	SI2	61.0	58.0	2757	6.15	6.12	3.74
53939	53940	0.75	Ideal	D	SI2	62.2	55.0	2757	5.83	5.87	3.64

```
print(type(df))
<class 'pandas. core.frame.DataFrame'>

df.shape
(53940, 11)
df. columns
Index(['Column_1', 'carat', 'cut', 'color', 'clarity', 'depth', 'table',
'price', 'x', 'y', 'z'],
dtype='object')
df. dtypes
Column_1 int64
carat float64
cut object
color object
clarity object
depth float64
table float64
price int64
x float64
y float64
z float64
dtype: object
```

```
print(df.info ())
<class 'pandas. core.frame.DataFrame'>
RangeIndex: 53940 entries, 0 to 53939

Data columns (total 11 columns):
# Column Non-Null Count Dtype
--- ------ -------------- -----
0 Column_1 53940 non-null int64
1 carat 53940 non-null float64
2 cut 53940 non-null object
3 color 53940 non-null object
4 clarity 53940 non-null object
5 depth 53940 non-null float64
6 table 53940 non-null float64
7 price 53940 non-null int64
8 x 53940 non-null float64
9 y 53940 non-null float64
10 z 53940 non-null float64
dtypes: float64(6), int64(2), object(3)
memory usage: 4.5+ MB
None
```

```
X=df.drop('price',axis=1)
X.head(10)
```

	Column_1	carat	cut	color	clarity	depth	table	x	y	z
0	1	0.23	Ideal	E	SI2	61.5	55.0	3.95	3.98	2.43
1	2	0.21	Premium	E	SI1	59.8	61.0	3.89	3.84	2.31
2	3	0.23	Good	E	VS1	56.9	65.0	4.05	4.07	2.31
3	4	0.29	Premium	I	VS2	62.4	58.0	4.20	4.23	2.63
4	5	0.31	Good	J	SI2	63.3	58.0	4.34	4.35	2.75
5	6	0.24	Very Good	J	VVS2	62.8	57.0	3.94	3.96	2.48
6	7	0.24	Very Good	I	VVS1	62.3	57.0	3.95	3.98	2.47
7	8	0.26	Very Good	H	SI1	61.9	55.0	4.07	4.11	2.53
8	9	0.22	Fair	E	VS2	65.1	61.0	3.87	3.78	2.49
9	10	0.23	Very Good	H	VS1	59.4	61.0	4.00	4.05	2.39

```
Y=df['price']
Y.head(10)
```

```
0 326
1 326
2 327
3 334
4 335
5 336
6 336
7 337
8 337
9 338
Name: price, dtype: int64
```

Preprocessing the Entire Data Set

Before training the machine learning models, it is critical to check the data for missing values, outliers, and noisy data and deal with them. The process of dealing with these issues is known as **data preprocessing**. If these issues are not resolved, it may lead to unrealistic assumptions by the models and may result in less accurate final models and also unrealistic predictions.

There are different types of data present in a data set. The data are not always numerical but may contain nominal or ordinal data. It is a good idea to transform the data in different ways during preprocessing and test different transformations in different models. This helps to select the right transformation for the model.

The example below demonstrates how to check for missing values in each feature of the data set.

1. **Load the data set *diamonds* and create the features and target matrices. This set contains nine features and one target. The steps are explained here.**

   ```
   import seaborn as sns
   diamonds=sns. load_dataset('diamonds')
   ```

2. Create the feature and target matrices and print the shape (number of rows and columns).

X=diamonds[['carat','cut','color','clarity','depth','table','x','y','z']]

Y = diamonds['price']

X.shape

(53940, 9)

3. **Check for missing values in all the features.**

print ("Carat:" + str(X['carat']. isnull (). sum ()))

print ("Cut:" + str(X['cut']. isnull (). sum ()))

print ("Color:" + str(X['color']. isnull (). sum ()))

print ("Clarity:" + str(X['clarity']. isnull (). sum ()))

print ("Depth:" + str(X['depth']. isnull (). sum ()))

print ("Table:" + str(X['table']. isnull (). sum ()))

print ("X:" + str(X['x']. isnull (). sum ()))

print ("Y:" + str(X['y']. isnull (). sum ()))

print ("Z: "+ str(X['z']. isnull (). sum ()))

Carat: 0

Cut: 0

Color: 0

Clarity: 0

Depth: 0

Table: 0

X: 0

Y: 0

Z: 0

The results above show that there are no missing values in any of the features.

Outliers and Missing Values in Data Sets (Messy Data)

A data set that has missing values, or has outliers, is considered as messy data set. The outliers are usually very small or large value in a data set that are unusual information. It is important to deal with these issues using data preprocessing or transformation. It is not unusual to find all missing values from one or more instances or where some instances or features have a few values missing.

To deal with the missing data, the usual convention that is followed is to eliminate the total row or the instance if all the features in that instance are missing values. On the other hand, if a feature has several values missing (5 to 10 percent) then these values should be replaced with values using the following two methods: (1) replace the missing values using the mean or median of the values of that feature if the feature has numerical values or (2) replace the missing values with the predicted values obtained using a regression function. Method (1) is known as **mean imputation** and method (2) is **regression imputation**.

Outliers

As indicated, outliers are values that are very large or very small. One way of detecting outliers is based on the Gaussian or Normal distribution. If the data values follow a normal distribution, the values outside of

[mean $\pm 3*$(standard deviation)] or $(\mu \pm \sigma)$ are considered outliers.

Once the outliers are detected, there are three ways to handle them:

1. Delete the outliers: sometimes, the outliers may result because of data recording errors. It is a good idea to delete them to avoid skewing the data.
2. Assign a new value: a new value may be assigned to the outliers using either the mean imputation or regression imputation. Here, we provide an example of missing values in a data set.

The data set used is Diamond which is a CSV file.

1. Open Jupyter Notebook.
2. Load the **Diamond** data set and store it in a variable called Diamond. Use the following code.
   import pandas as pd
   Diamond=pd.read_csv ("C:\\Users\\asahay\\OneDrive -
   \\Desktop\\Diamond.csv")
   Diamond.head(15)

	Column_1	carat	cut	color	clarity	depth	table	price	x	y	z
0	1	0.23	Ideal	E	SI2	61.5	55.0	326.0	3.95	3.98	2.43
1	2	0.21	Premium	E	SI1	59.8	61.0	326.0	3.89	3.84	2.31
2	3	0.23	Good	E	VS1	56.9	65.0	327.0	4.05	4.07	2.31
3	4	0.29	Premium	I	VS2	62.4	58.0	334.0	4.20	4.23	2.63
4	5	0.31	Good	J	SI2	NaN	58.0	335.0	4.34	4.35	2.75
5	6	0.24	Very Good	J	VVS2	62.8	57.0	336.0	3.94	3.96	2.48
6	7	0.24	Very Good	I	VVS1	62.3	57.0	336.0	3.95	3.98	2.47
7	8	0.26	Very Good	H	SI1	61.9	55.0	337.0	4.07	4.11	2.53
8	9	0.22	Fair	E	VS2	65.1	61.0	337.0	3.87	3.78	2.49
9	10	0.23	Very Good	H	VS1	59.4	61.0	NaN	4.00	4.05	2.39
10	11	0.30	Good	J	SI1	64.0	55.0	339.0	4.25	4.28	2.73
11	12	0.23	Ideal	J	VS1	62.8	56.0	340.0	3.93	3.90	2.46
12	13	0.22	Premium	F	SI1	60.4	61.0	342.0	3.88	3.84	2.33
13	14	0.31	Ideal	J	SI2	62.2	54.0	NaN	4.35	4.37	2.71
14	15	0.20	Premium	E	SI2	NaN	62.0	345.0	3.79	3.75	2.27

3. Create a variable called **price** to store the value of this feature from the data set. Print out the top 15 values of the **price** variable.

price= Diamond['price']

price. Head (15)

0 326.0

1 326.0

2 327.0

3 334.0

4 335.0

5 336.0

6 336.0

7 337.0

8 337.0

9 **NaN**

10 339.0

11 340.0

12 342.0

13 **NaN**

14 345.0

Name: price, dtype: float64

4. Check the shape of the price variable.

price. shape

(53940,)

5. The price variable has Not a Number (**NaN**) values in rows 9 and 13. These are considered missing values.

6. Count the number of missing values (NaN Vlues) in the variable **price** using the isnull() function.

price. Isnull ().sum()

2

The result shows that there are two missing values in the feature **price** of the **Diamond** data set.

7. As explained above, create a variable called **depth** to store the value of this feature from the data set. Print out the top 15 values of the **depth** variable.

depth= Diamond['depth']

depth. head(15)

0 61.5

1 59.8

2 56.9

3 62.4

4 NaN

5 62.8

6 62.3

7 61.9

8 65.1

9 59.4

10 64.0

11 62.8

12 60.4

13 62.2

14 NaN

Name: depth, dtype: float64

8. Check the shape of the feature **depth** and count the number of missing or NaN values in this feature.

depth. shape

(53940,)

depth. isnull().sum()

2

As we can see, the feature **depth** also has two missing values that are not numbers. It is also evident that the missing values in this feature are 2 out of 53,940 instances. This is negligible but these values can be replaced using mean imputation. This means that we will calculate the mean of the feature *depth* and replace all the missing values with the mean. Follow the steps below:

9. Calculate the mean of the feature depth and round the mean value to one decimal place.

mean=depth. mean ( )

mean

61.74940487225996

print ("The value rounded to 1 decimal value", round(mean,1))

The value rounded to 1 decimal value 61.7

10. Replace the missing values with mean. Use fillna () function. To check that the values are replaced, print the first 15 values.

depth. fillna (mean, inplace=True)

depth. head (15)

The result should show that the NaN values in the feature **depth** are replaced with the mean.

Outliers: As indicated, outliers are values that are very large or very small. One way of detecting outliers is based on the Gaussian or Normal distribution. If the data values follow a normal distribution, the values outside of

[mean $\pm$ 3*(standard deviation)] or ($\mu \pm \sigma$)] are considered outliers. (A)

Once the outliers are detected, there are three ways to handle them: (1) Delete the outliers: sometimes, the outliers may result because of data recording errors. It is a good idea to delete them to avoid skewing the data.

To detect the outliers in the variable **depth,** first, we will create a histogram of the feature *depth*. This will visually provide some ideas on the outliers. We use *matplotlib* to plot the **histogram** of the feature **depth**. Continue with the steps below. (Note: the steps continue from Step 10 above.)

11. Import Matplotlib and plot a histogram of the **depth** variable using **hist** () function. Type the following:

import matplotlib. pyplot as plt

plt. hist(depth)

plt. show ()

The resulting histogram is shown in Figure 5.1. The shape of the histogram can be well approximated by a Gaussian or Normal distribution. Therefore, the outliers can be determined using Equation (A).

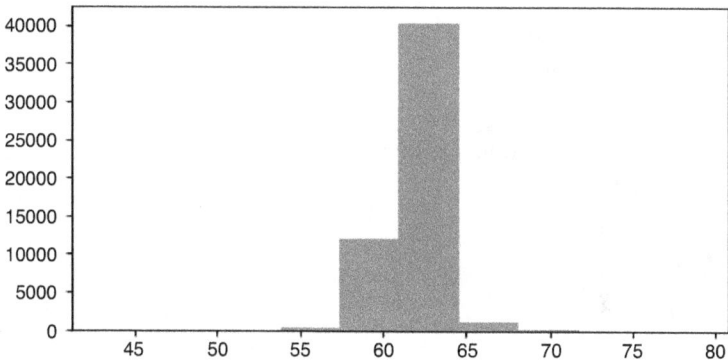

Figure 5.1 Histogram from Matplotlib

To determine the outliers in the variable **depth**, we will use [mean ±3*(standard deviations)].

12. The minimum value is found by calculating the mean of the values in the variable *depth* and subtracting three standard deviations from it using the following code. The minimum value will be stored in a variable, **min_val.** Use the following code.

min_val=depth. mean () - (3*depth.std())

min_val

57.45155450801473

The minimum value is printed above.

13. In a similar way, the maximum value will be calculated and stored in a variable, **man_val.** Use the following code.

```
max_val=depth. mean()+(3*depth.std())
max_val
66.0472552365052
```

The maximum value is printed above.

From the above, the minimum value is 57.452 and the maximum value is 66.047. This indicates that there are no outliers at the lower tail of the distribution (see the histogram). The maximum value in the variable depth is 66.047. This indicates that there are values outside of the maximum values.

14. We will count the number of instances that are above the maximum value. Using indexing, we calculate the values in the variable **depth** that are above the maximum value and store them in available named outliers. Use the following code:

```
outliers=depth[depth>max_val]
outliers. count ()
366
```

A partial list of outliers is shown as follows.

```
97 66.3
204 67.9
298 67.4
352 67.3
369 66.4
...
53495 66.9
53540 72.9
53727 66.9
53800 68.7
53863 66.8
Name: depth, Length: 366, dtype: float64
```

The total number of outliers is 366. This is less than 1 percent of the total number of instances 53,940. The number of outliers is significantly smaller, they can be deleted. We will delete the instances from the variable **depth.**

15. Redefine the values stored in the variable **depth** using indexing and calculate only the values below the max_val threshold and print the shape of **depth**.

depth=depth[depth<=max_val]

depth. shape

(53572,)

This shows that the outliers are deleted and the total number of instances in depth is now reduced by the number of outliers. Note that the total number of instances in the **Diamond** data set is 53,940 and there are 366 outliers. The final number of instances reported is 53,572, which is two more. This is because there are two feature values labeled NaN.

Dealing With Categorical Features

In a data set, it is not unusual to find categorical features. The data set with categorical or qualitative variables are not numbers and they are classified as **nominal** or **ordinal**. The nominal data are the data that are classified in a category where there is no order involved. An example of such data is the color of your car or marital status. Since there is no order involved, this type of data cannot be ranked, and it is difficult to which value is bigger or better. The other type of categorical data is ordinal. These are also not numbers but there is some order involved. An example of this type of data is the student grades that are usually classified as A, B, C, and so on. These are categorical but there is order involved. For example, the letter grade A is better than B, B is better than C, and so on.

The data set having categorical features may be text instead of numbers. In creating machine learning models, the categorical features are transformed into numeric values. This makes the model training efficient, resulting in faster running time and better model performance.

The process by which the categorical variables are converted into numerical values is known as **label encoding**. This process is referred to as **feature engineering**, which generates a label encoding that assigns a numeric value to each category. This value replaces the category in the data set. We will demonstrate the feature engineering and label encoding using the Diamond data set that we have used earlier.

We will use the Diamond.csv file using pandas and explore the categorical feature that we will code.

1. Import Pandas then import **Scikit Learns's Label Encoder** ().
   import pandas as pd
   from sklearn. preprocessing import LabelEncoder
2. Download the **Dimond.cvs file**.
   Diamond=pd.read_csv ("Diamonds.csv")
3. You may use the describe command to calculate the descriptive statistics of the numeric features. (The output of this command is not shown here.)
   Diamond.describe()
   Diamond.head()

	Column_1	carat	cut	color	clarity	depth	table	price	x	y	z
0	1	0.23	Ideal	E	SI2	61.5	55.0	326	3.95	3.98	2.43
1	2	0.21	Premium	E	SI1	59.8	61.0	326	3.89	3.84	2.31
2	3	0.23	Good	E	VS1	56.9	65.0	327	4.05	4.07	2.31
3	4	0.29	Premium	I	VS2	62.4	58.0	334	4.20	4.23	2.63
4	5	0.31	Good	J	SI2	63.3	58.0	335	4.34	4.35	2.75

By printing the first five instances, it is evident that the feature *cut* is a categorical variable.

4. Use the command below to see the different categories of the feature *cut*.
   Diamond["cut"]. unique ()
   array (['Ideal', 'Premium', 'Good', 'Very Good', 'Fair'], dtype=object)

   lbl_encode=LabelEncoder ()
   lbl_encode.fit_transform (Diamond['cut'])
   array([2, 3, 1, ..., 4, 3, 2])
   Diamond['cut_label']=lbl_encode.fit_transform(Diamond["cut"])
   Diamond["cut_label"].value_counts()
   2 21551

3 13791

4 12082

1 4906

0 1610

Name: cut_label, dtype: int64

Diamond['cut'].value_counts ()

Ideal 21551

Premium 13791

Very Good 12082

Good 4906

Fair 1610

Name: cut, dtype: int64

Data Preprocessing (Normalization, Standardization)

Normalization

Data normalization in machine learning is a part of data preprocessing and data preparation. Normalization involves rescaling the values of all the features so that they lie in the range of 0 and 1 with a maximum of 1. The equation to normalize the values of a feature is given by:

$$Z_i = \frac{\min(x)}{\max(x) - \min(x)}$$

where Z_i is the ith normalized value and x_i are the data values.

Data normalization reorganizes the data so that it can be used uniformly and is similar for further analysis. It is a process of data cleaning by eliminating redundant and unstructured data and making the data appear uniform across all features. To normalize a data set, the data need to be scaled to a common range, such as between 0 and 1. This is done using the method of Min–Max scaling or Z-score normalization as shown above. Normalization reduces data redundancy, improves data analysis, and enhances data security. It can eliminate errors, inconsistencies, and missing values that can affect the accuracy of data and analysis.

Standardization

Data standardization is a rescaling technique. It transforms the data into a Gaussian distribution with mean equals zero and standard deviation of 1. The following equation shows the standardization process of features in a data set.

$$Z_i = \frac{x_i - \text{mean}(x)}{\text{std}(x)}$$

where Z_i is the ith standardized value and x_i are the data values.

Data standardization is a data preprocessing technique in many machine learning models. It is used to standardize the range of features of an input data set.

Data standardization is used when features of the input data set have large variations or differences between their ranges, or when the data are measured using different scales of measurement, for example, pounds, kilograms, meters, feet, and so on.

These differences in the ranges of initial features cause trouble for many machine learning models. For example, suppose a model is based on distance computation, if one of the features has a large range or variation, the distance will be governed by this particular feature. Using data standardization, the data are converted to **a standard format that is easily understood and processed by computers**.

As an example, suppose we want to predict the outcome of a complex system using neural networks. The target or the dependent variable values range between 0 and 12,000. Also, different features or independent variables have wide ranges. Suppose all the variables have approximately Gaussian distribution. In such cases, it is important to scale the data before training the model. One way is to use the Z-score. Note: Both the normalization and standardization techniques can be implemented using Seaborn in Jupyter Notebook.

Summary

Data is one of the most critical parts of creating and implementing machine learning models. In this chapter, we demonstrated, through several examples, how to get the data for analysis. Before data can be used to create models, it must be checked and preprocessed for accuracy. We showed how to import data sets using Python and Seaborn packages in Jupyter Notebook. This chapter showed the ways to load the data for analysis, to create the features and target matrix, and how to perform some data visualizations and perform exploratory data analysis (EDA). Through stepwise instructions, the data manipulation process, such as checking the data for validity, was shown. The last section of this chapter discussed the data preprocessing techniques including normalization and standardization. The importance and needs for data normalization and standardization were explained.

CHAPTER 6

Supervised Learning Models

Chapter Highlights

Supervised Learning Models and Applications
- Supervised and Unsupervised Learning Comparison

Regression Models
- Linear Models: Univariate Linear Regression Model
  $Y = w_0 + w_1 x$
- Least Squares Method, Interpretation of Models, the Standard Error of Estimate, Coefficient of Determination R^2
- Multivariate Regression Models—n Explanatory Variables
- Ridge Regression, Multicollinearity and Autocorrelation, Effects of Multicollinearity,
- Nonlinear regression (Quadratic Regression)
- Other Types of Regression Algorithms Lasso and Ridge Regressions
- L1 and L2 Regularizations, Metrics to Quantify Performance (MSE, R^2 Value, and so on)

Classification Models
- Statistical Binary Classification
- Logistic regression—Binary Response Variable
- Linear Discriminant Analysis (LDA)
- Support Vector Machines—Hyperplane and Kernelling
- Classification and Regression Trees (CART), Decision Trees
- Multivariate Classification Models
- Naïve Bayes Classifier, k-Nearest Neighbor (KNN)
- Random Forest Classifier

Summary

Introduction

Machine learning applications revolve around ***algorithms.*** An algorithm is a set of operations, procedures, or equations used to solve a problem. Algorithms may be seen as input–output processes that process data through a series of well-defined rules. The objective is to produce an output that is often the solution to a problem. The algorithms take input in the form of data and define the output. The input in the algorithms processes the data through a language or computer program that defines and executes functions to come to a solution or produce an output.

Machine learning algorithms and models are divided into these main categories: (1) **supervised learning**, (2) **unsupervised learning,** (3) **semisupervised learning**, and (4) **reinforcement learning.** Figure 6.1 summarizes these models.

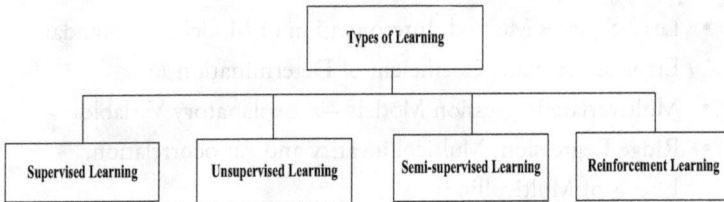

```
                        ┌─────────────────┐
                        │ Types of Learning│
                        └─────────────────┘
       ┌──────────────┬──────────┴──────────┬──────────────────┐
┌──────────────┐ ┌──────────────┐ ┌──────────────────┐ ┌──────────────────────┐
│ Supervised   │ │ Unsupervised │ │ Semi-supervised  │ │ Reinforcement Learning│
│ Learning     │ │ Learning     │ │ Learning         │ │                      │
└──────────────┘ └──────────────┘ └──────────────────┘ └──────────────────────┘
```

Figure 6.1 Supervised learning models

Supervised Learning

In supervised learning, the algorithm learns from example data and the given output or target. The data contains the features or independent variables and the dependent variable also known as the label or the target. It is a machine learning technique that is widely used in various fields such as engineering, finance, business, health care, sales, marketing predictions, and more. In this type of machine learning, the algorithm is trained on labeled data or targets to make predictions or decisions based on the features or independent variables. In supervised learning problems, the algorithms learn a mapping between the input and output data. This mapping is learned from a labeled data set consisting of pairs of input and output data. The algorithm learns the relationship between the input and output data that is used to make predictions on new, unseen data.

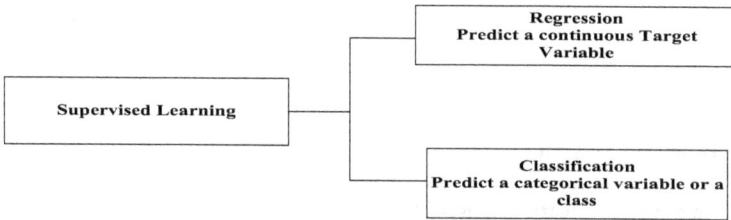

Figure 6.2 Types of supervised learning models

The data consist of input or features and corresponding output labels. The predictions are made using the input features that are attributes or characteristics of the data. The output labels are the desired outcomes or targets that the algorithm predicts.

The two main types of supervised learning are regression and classification problems (Figure 6.2). The target in regression problems is a numeric value, whereas classification problems have targets that are string labels, qualitative or categorical variables, such as class. An example of a regression problem may be to determine the sales for a company based on advertising dollars and other features. The goal of a classification problem would be to determine whether a loan granted by a bank may result in a default based on the customer's credit history, education level, age, marital status, and other available factors.

In supervised learning problems, the computer is presented with example inputs and their desired outputs by the analyst, and the goal is to create a model to learn a general rule that maps inputs to outputs. The supervised learning method is similar to human learning under the supervision of a teacher.

The learning involves creating a model by establishing the relationship between inputs or the *features* and the desired output or some *target*. Once this model is established, it can be used to apply labels to new, unknown data to predict future events. The idea is to learn from the past data and apply it to new data to make predictions for the future events using the created learning algorithm. The output from the learning algorithm can also compare its output to the known output to find the associated error that helps modify the model.

Supervised learning has been used to create complex models that are used to make accurate predictions on new data. The models using supervised learning require large amounts of labeled training data to be effective. The quality and quantity of training data determine the accuracy of the model.

Training the System

The first step in creating machine learning algorithms (including supervised and unsupervised learning models) is training the model. In the training process, the data are usually split in the ratio of 80:20 where 80 percent of the data are used to train the model and the rest is used as testing data. This 80:20 is not always used as a definite rule. It is recommended that the data should be split into three sets—training, validation, and test sets. We explained this in Chapter 3.

The model learns from training data where the learning means that the model uses some logic of its own for the learning process. Once the model is trained, the next step is to test the model. For testing, the input uses the remaining 20 percent of data that the model has never used before. The model makes a prediction using the model which is compared to the actual output and calculates the accuracy of the model.

Simple Supervised Machine Learning Models

Here we describe some regression models. In regression problems, the target variable is a continuous value. The goal of the regression models is to predict the value of the target variable based on the input variables or the features. There are different types of regression models, including simple linear regression, multiple regression, nonlinear regression, polynomial regression, ridge regression, and other variations. Other associated metrics, such as regularization, are used to quantify the model performance. Some other metrics used to assess the regression models are mean square error (MSE), R^2 value, and several others that we have discussed in Chapter 3.

Linear Models—Univariate Linear Regression

$$Y = w_0 + w_1 x$$

This is one of the simplest supervised learning models. It involves establishing and understanding the relationship between a feature and a target value.

In general, we have one *target* or *response* variable, y and one or more *features*, x_1, x_2, ..., x_k. These features are also called *predictors*. If there is only one feature that we are trying to relate to the target, then this is a case of *simple regression*. On the other hand, if we have two or more features that are related to a target then we have a case of *multiple regression*. In this section, we will discuss simple regression. In regression analysis, the relationship between the target and feature or features are described by a mathematical model known as a *regression model* shown below. This model can then be used to make predictions with new data.

Equation (6.1) shows the relationship between the values of the feature, x and the target, y or the independent and dependent variable and an error term.

$$y = w_0 + w_1 x + \varepsilon \quad (6.1)$$

where y = dependent variable, x = independent variable,
$w_0 = y$ - intercept (population), w_1 = slope of the population regression line, and
ε = random error term (ε is the Greek letter *epsilon*).

The regression model is described in the form of a regression equation that is obtained using the *least squares method*. In a simple linear regression, the form of the regression equation is $y = w_0 + w_1 x$. This is the equation of a straight line in the slope-intercept form.

We will illustrate the least squares method using an example. Suppose that the sales manager of a company is interested in the relationship between advertising expenditure and sales. He has good reasons to believe that an increase in advertising dollars leads to increased sales. The manager has the sales and advertising data from 15 different regions, as shown in Table 6.1. To investigate the relationship between the sales and advertisement expenditures, a scatter plot was created that visually depicts the possible relationship between two variables.

An investigation of the plot in Figure 6.3 shows a positive relationship between the sales and advertising expenditure therefore, the manager would like to predict the sales (target) using the advertising expenditure (the feature) using a simple regression model.

Table 6.1 Sales and advertisement data

Sales ($1000s)	Advertising ($1000s)
458	34
390	30
378	29
426	30
330	26
400	31
458	33
410	30
628	41
553	38
728	44
498	40
708	48
719	47
658	45

From Figure 6.3, it can be seen that the plotted points can be well approximated by a straight line of the form $y = w_0 + w_1 x$, where w_0 and w_1 are the y-intercept and the slope of the line. The process of estimating this regression equation uses a widely used mathematical tool known as the **least squares method.**

The least squares method requires fitting a line through the data points so that the sum of the squares of errors or residuals is a minimum. These errors or residuals are the vertical distances of the points from the fitted line. Thus, the least squares method determines the best fitting line through the data points that ensures that the sum of the squares of the vertical distances or deviations from the given points and the fitted line is a minimum.

Figure 6.4 shows the concept of the least squares method. The figure shows a line fitted to the scatter plot of Figure 6.3 using the least squares method. This line is the estimated line denoted using y-hat ($\hat{y}$). The method of estimating this line will be illustrated later. The equation of this line is given as follows.

$$\hat{y} = -150.9 + 18.33x$$

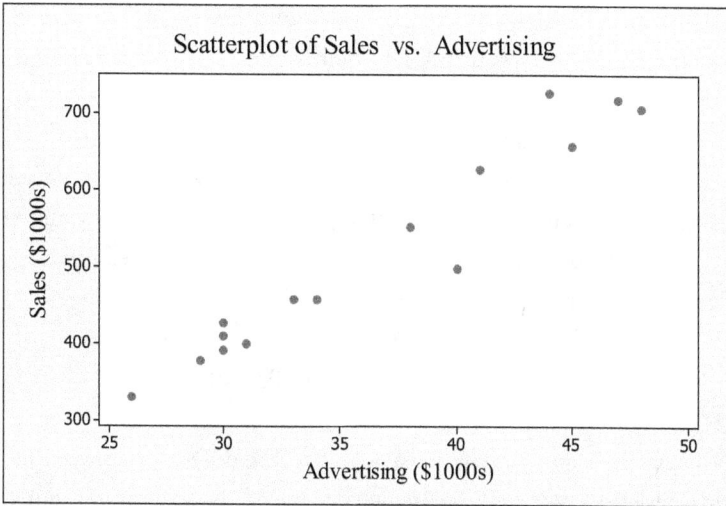

Figure 6.3 Scatterplot of sales and advertisement expenditures

The vertical distance of each point from the line is known as the *error or residual*. Note that the residual or error of a point can be positive, negative, or zero depending upon whether the point is above, below, or on the fitted line. If the point is above the line, the error is positive, whereas if the point is below the fitted line, the error is negative.

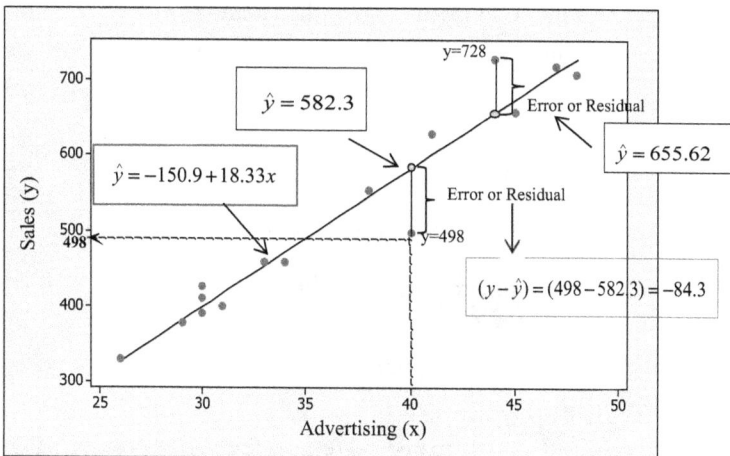

Figure 6.4 Fitting the regression line to the sales and advertising data of Table 6.1

Figure 6.4 shows graphically the errors for a few points. To demon-strate how the error or residual for a point is calculated, refer to the data in Table 6.1.

Table 6.1 shows that for the advertising expenditure of 40 ($x = 40$) the sales are 498 or ($y = 498$). This is shown graphically in Figure 6.4. The estimated or predicted sales for $x = 40$ equals the vertical distance all the way up to the fitted regression line from $y = 498$. This predicted value can be determined using the equation of the fitted line as

$$\hat{y} = -150.9 + 18.33x = 150.9 + 18.33(40) = 582.3$$

This is shown in Figure 6.4 as $\hat{y} = 582.3$. The difference between the observed sales, $y = 498$, and the predicted value of y is the error or residual and is equal to

$$(\hat{y} - y) = (498 - 582.3) = -84.3$$

The errors for the other observed values can be calculated in a similar way. The vertical deviation of a point from the fitted regression line rep-resents the amount of error associated with that point. The least squares method determines the values w_0 and w_1 in the fitted regression line $\hat{y} = w_0 + w_1 x$ that will minimize the sum of the squares of the errors. Mini-mizing the sum of the squares of the errors provides a unique line through the data points such that the distance of each point from the fitted line is a minimum.

Interpreting the Fitted Regression Line

This equation for the estimated regression line:

$$\hat{y} = -150.9 + 18.33x$$

The slope (b_1) of the estimated regression line has a positive value of 18.33. This means that as the advertising expenditures (x) increase, the sales increase. Since the advertising expenditures (x) and the sales both are measured in $1,000s, the estimated regression equation,

$\hat{y} = -150.9 + 18.33x$, means that each unit increase in the value of x (or every $1,000 increase in the advertising expenditures) will lead to an increase of $18,330 (or 18.33*1,000 = 18,330) in expected sales.

We can also use the regression equation to predict the sales for a given value of x or the advertisement expenditure. For instance, the predicted sales for $x = 40$ can be calculated as:

$$\hat{y} = -150.9 + 18.33(40) = 582.3$$

Thus, for the advertising expenditure of $40,000, the predicted sales would be $582,300.

The Standard Error of the Estimate (s)

The standard error of the estimate (s) measures the variation or scatter of the points around the fitted line of regression. This is measured in units of the response variable (y). The standard error of the estimate is analogous to the standard deviation. The standard deviation measures the variability around the mean, whereas the standard error of the estimate (s) measures the variability around the fitted line of regression. A large value of s indicates a larger variation of the points around the fitted line of regression.

The Coefficient of Determination (r^2) and Its Meaning

The coefficient of determination, r^2 is an indication of how well the independent variable predicts the dependent variable. In other words, it is used to judge the adequacy of the regression model. The value of r^2 lies between 0 and 1 ($0 \leq r^2 \leq 1$) or 0 to 100 percent. The closer the value of r^2 to 1 or 100 percent, the better is the model because the r^2 value indicates the amount of variation in the data explained by the regression model.

The coefficient of determination, r^2 is used to measure the goodness of fit for the regression equation. It measures the variation in y explained by the variation in the independent variable x, or r^2 is the ratio of the explained variation to the total variation. A computer printout showing the solution to the problem is shown in Table 6.2.

Table 6.2 Computer solution of a regression problem

Regression Equation

Sales	=	-150.9+ 18.33 Ad.

Coefficients

Term	Coef	SE Coef	T-Value	P-Value	VIF
Constant	-150.9	46.7	-3.23	0.007	
Ad.	18.33	1.26	14.56	0.000	1.00
Total		14	266454		

Model Summary

S	R-sq	R-sq(adj)	R-sq(pred)
34.4067	94.22%	93.78%	92.60%

Multivariate Linear Regression—*n* Explanatory Variables

$$y = w_0 + w_1 x_1 + w_2 x_2 + \ldots + w_n x_n = \sum_{i=0}^{n} w_i x_i$$

Multiple linear regression is one of the most widely used prediction techniques used in machine learning. Multiple regression enables us to explore the relationship between a response variable or target, and two or more features or predictors.

Multiple Regression Model

The multiple regression describes the relationship between the target and two or more features. The mathematical form of a multiple linear regression model relating the target y and two or more features $x_1, x_2, \ldots x_k$ with the associated error term is given by:

$$y = w_0 + w_1 x_1 + w_2 x_2 + \ldots + w_n x_n + \varepsilon \quad (6.2)$$

where $x_1, x_2, \ldots x_k$ are n features (independent or explanatory variables), $w_0, w_1, w_2, \ldots w_n$ are the regression coefficients, and ε is the associated error term. Equation (6.2) can be viewed as a ***population multiple regression model*** in which y is a linear function of unknown parameters $w_0, w_1, w_2, \ldots w_n$ and an error term, ε. The error ε explains the variability in y that cannot be explained by the linear effects of the independent variables. The multiple regression model is similar to the simple regression model except that multiple regression involves more than one feature.

In a multiple regression, the least squares method determines the best fitting plane or the hyperplane through the data points that ensures that the sum of the squares of the vertical distances or deviations from the given points and the plane are a minimum.

Computer Analysis of Multiple Regression

In this section, we provide a computer analysis of multiple regression. Due to the complexity involved in computation, computer software is always used to model and solve regression problems. We discuss the steps using MINITAB and EXCEL. The problem is explained.

Problem: The home heating cost is believed to be related to the average outside temperature, the size of the house, and the age of the heating furnace. A multiple regression model is to be fitted to investigate the relationship between the heating cost and the three predictors or independent variables. The data in Table 6.3 show the home heating cost (y), average temperature (x_1), house size (x_2) in thousands of square feet, and the age of the furnace (x_3) in years. The home heating cost is the response variable, and the other three variables are predictors. (The data for this problem are also available in the MINITAB data file: HEAT_COST. MTW, and EXCEL data file: HEAT_COST.xlsx).

Table 6.4 shows the result of running the multiple regression using MINITAB. In this table, we have marked some of the calculations (e.g., b_0, b_1, s_{bo}, s_{b1} for clarity and explanation). These are not a part of the computer output. Refer to the *regression analysis* part of Table 6.2 for further analysis.

The analysis and interpretation of the computer results are provided below.

Table 6.3 Home heating cost data

Obs.	Avg. Temp.	House Size	Age of Furnace	Heating Cost ($)
1	37	3	6	210
2	30	4	9	365
3	37	2.5	4	182
4	61	1	3	65
5	66	2	5	82
6	39	3.5	4	205
7	15	4.1	6	360
8	8	3.8	9	295
9	22	2.9	10	235
10	56	2.2	4	125
11	55	2	3	78
12	40	3.8	4	162
13	21	4.5	12	405
14	40	5	6	325
15	61	1.8	5	82
16	21	4.2	7	277
17	63	2.3	2	99
18	41	3	10	195
19	28	4.2	7	240
20	31	3	4	144
21	33	3.2	4	265
22	31	4.2	11	355
23	36	2.8	3	175
24	56	1.2	4	57
25	35	2.3	8	196
26	36	3.6	6	215
27	9	4.3	8	380
28	10	4	11	300
29	21	3	9	240
30	51	2.5	7	130

Table 6.4 MINITAB regression analysis results

Regression Analysis: Heating Cost Versus Avg. Temp., House Size, and so on

The regression equation is
Heating Cost = 44.4 - 1.65 Avg. Temp. + 57.5 House Size + 7.91 Age of Furnace

```
Predictor Coef SE Coef T P

Constant 44.39 (w₀) 59.07 (s_b0) 0.75 0.459

Avg. Temp. -1.6457 (w₁) 0.6967 (s_b1) -2.36 0.026

House Size 57.46 (w₂) 10.35 (s_b2) 5.55 0.000

Age of Furnace 7.908 (w₃) 3.294 (s_b3) 2.40 0.024
```

$\longrightarrow$ Regression Coefficients are Sb0, Sb1, Sb2, Sb3

`S = 37.3174 R-Sq = 88.0% R-Sq(adj) = 86.6%`

Analysis of Variance SSE

$\swarrow$

```
Source DF SS MS F P

Regression 3 265777 88592 63.62 0.000

Residual Error 26 36207 1393

Total 29 301985
```

The Regression Equation

Since there are three independent or explanatory variables, the regression equation is of the form:

$$y = w_0 + w_1 x_1 + w_2 x_2 + ... + w_3 x_3$$

The regression equation from Table 14.2:

Heating Cost = 44.4 – 1.65 Avg. Temp. + 57.5
House Size + 7.91 Age of Furnace (6.3)

or

$$\hat{y} = -44.4 - 1.65x_1 + 57.5x_2\ 7.91x_3\ (6.4)$$

where y is the response variable (Heating Cost), x_1, x_2, x_3 are the independent variables as described earlier, the regression coefficients w_0, w_1, w_2, ... w_n are stored under the column **Coef** (see Table 6.4). In the regression equation, these coefficients appear in rounded form.

The regression equation can be stated in the form of Equation (6.3) or (6.4), which are the estimated regression equations relating the heating cost to all three independent variables.

Interpreting the Regression Equation

Equation (6.3) or (6.4) can be interpreted in the following way:

- $b_1 = -1.65$ means that for each unit increase in the average temperature (x_1), the heating cost y (in dollars) can be predicted to go down by 1.65 (or, $1.65) when the house size (x_2), and the age of the furnace (x_3) are held constant.
- $b_2 = +57.5$ means that for each unit increase in the house size $(x_2$ in thousands of square feet), the heating cost, y (in dollars) can be predicted to go up by 57.5 when the average temperature (x_1) and the age of the furnace (x_3) are held constant.
- $b_3 = +7.91$ means that for each unit increase in the age of the furnace $(x_3$ in years), the heating cost y can be predicted to go up by $7.91 when the average temperature (x_1) and the house size (x_2) are held constant.

Standard Error of the Estimate (s) and Its Meaning

The standard error of the estimate or the standard deviation of the model S is a measure of scatter or the measure of the variation of the points around the regression hyperplane. A small value of S is desirable for a good regression model. The estimation of y is more accurate for smaller values of S. The value of the standard error of estimate is reported in the regression analysis (see Table 14.2). This value is measured in terms of the response variable (y). For this example, the standard error of the estimate,

$$s = 37.32 \text{ dollars}$$

The standard error of the estimate is used to check the utility of the model and to provide a measure of the reliability of the prediction made from the model. One interpretation of s is that the interval $\pm 2s$ will provide an approximation to the accuracy with which the regression model will predict the future value of the response y for given values of x. Thus, for our example, we can expect the model to provide predictions of heating cost (y) to be within $\pm 2s = \pm 2(37.32) = \pm 74.64$ dollars.

Error Variance

The error variance σ_0^2 is an estimate of the population error variance and is denoted by s^2. The error variance σ_0^2 can be calculated using the following formula:

$$\sigma_0^2 = \frac{\Sigma(y_i - \hat{y})^2}{n - (k - 1)} \quad (6.5)$$

In the above equation, $\Sigma(y_i - \hat{y})^2$ is the sum of the square of errors also known as SSE, n is the number of observations (n = 30 for our example), k is the number of independent variables (k = 3 for our example). The value of SSE is reported in the *Analysis of Variance* part of Table 14.2. From this table, **SSE = 36,207**.

The estimate of σ_0^2 for a multiple regression model in Equation (6.5) is denoted by s^2 and is calculated using:

$$s^2 = \frac{SSE}{n - (k + 1)} \quad (6.6)$$

The denominator in Equation (6.6); $n - (k+1) = n -$ (number of estimated β parameters). Since we must estimate four parameters $\beta_0, \beta_1, \beta_2, \beta_3$ in this example, the estimator of σ_0^2 is

$$s^2 = \frac{SSE}{n-(k+1)} = \frac{36207}{30-4} = 1392.58 \quad (6.7)$$

This value is also known as the *MSE* and is reported in the *analysis of variance* part of Table 6.2. From this table, the value of MSE can be read from *MS* column and *Residual Error* row and is 1,393. The estimate of σ_0 can be calculated as

$$s = \sqrt{1393} = 37.32$$

This value is reported as $s = 37.3172$ under the regression analysis in Table 6.4. The error variance (s^2) and the standard deviation or the standard error of estimate (s) are important quantities and are helpful in determining the prediction validity of the model. A large value of s^2 or s indicates a large error and will affect the prediction accuracy of the model, whereas a small value of s^2 or s is an indication of a more reliable model.

The Coefficient of Multiple Determination (r^2)

The coefficient of multiple determination is often used to check the adequacy of the regression model. The value of r^2 lies between 0 and 1, or 0 and 100 percent, that is, $0 \leq r^2 \leq 1$. It indicates the fraction of total variation of the dependent variable y that is explained by the independent variables or predictors. Usually, the closer the value of R^2 to 1 or 100 percent, the stronger is the model. However, one should be careful in drawing conclusions based solely on the value of r^2. A large value of r^2 does not necessarily mean that the model provides a good fit to the data. In the case of multiple regression, the addition of a new variable to the model always increases the value of r^2 even if the added variable is not statistically significant. Thus, the addition of a new variable will increase r^2 indicating a stronger model but may lead to poor predictions of new values.

In the above equations, SSE is the sum of square of errors (unexplained variation or error), SST is the total sum of squares, and SSR is the sum of squares due to regression (explained variation). These values can be read from the *analysis of variance* part of Table 6.4. From this table,

$$r^2 = \frac{SSR}{SST} = \frac{265777}{301985} = 0.88 \quad (6.8)$$

The value of r^2 is calculated and reported in the *regression analysis* part of Table 6.4. For our example, the coefficient of multiple determination; r^2 (reported as **R-sq**) is

$$r^2 = 88.0\%$$

This means that 88.0% of the variability in y is explained by the three independent variables used in the model. Note that $r^2 = 0$ implies a complete lack of fit of the model to the data, whereas $r^2 = 1$ implies a perfect fit.

The value of $r^2 = 88.0\%$ for our example implies that using the three independent variables: average temperature, size of the house, and the age of the furnace, in the model, 88.0% of the total variation in heating cost (y) can be explained. The statistic r^2 tells how well the model fits the data and thus, provides the overall predictive usefulness of the model.

The above examples of simple and multiple regressions can easily be implemented using Python.

Multicollinearity in Regression Models

We discussed linear regression that establishes a relationship between the target or dependent variable (Y) and one or more features or independent variables (X). Other types of regression models are used when the data suffer from multicollinearity (where independent variables are highly correlated).

Ridge regression is **the method to analyze multicollinearity in multiple regression data**. It is used when a data set contains a large number of predictor variables. We will discuss this method in subsequent sections.

Multicollinearity and Autocorrelation in Multiple Regression

Multicollinearity is a measure of correlation among the predictors in a regression model. Multicollinearity exists when two or more independent variables in the regression model are correlated with each other. In practice, it is not unusual to see correlations among the independent variables. However, if serious multicollinearity is present, it may cause problems by increasing the variance of the regression coefficients making them unstable and difficult to interpret. Also, highly correlated independent variables increase the likelihood of rounding errors in the calculation of β estimates and standard errors. In the presence of multicollinearity, the regression results may be misleading.

Effects of Multicollinearity

(a) Consider the regression model where the production cost (y) is related to three independent variables: machine hours (x_1), material cost (x_2), and labor hours (x_3):

$$y = w_0 + w_1 x_1 + w_2 x_2 + ... + w_3 x_3 \quad (6.9)$$

MINITAB computer output for this model is shown in Table 6.5. If we perform t-tests for testing β_1, β_2, and β_3, we find that all the three independent variables are nonsignificant at $\alpha = 0.05$, while the F-test for $H_0: \beta_1 = \beta_2 = \beta_3 = 0$ is significant (see *analysis of variance* results in Table 6.5 where $p = 0.000$). The results are contradictory, but in fact, they are not. The tests on individual b_i parameters indicate that the contribution of one variable, say x_1 = machine hours is not significant after the effects of x_2 = material cost, and x_3 = labor hours have been accounted for. However, the result of the F-test indicates that at least one of the three variables is significant or is making a contribution to the prediction of response y. It is also possible that at least two or all the three variables are contributing to the prediction of y. Here, the contribution of one variable is overlapping with that of the other variable or variables. This is because of the multicollinearity effect.

(b) Multicollinearity may also have an effect on the signs of the parameter estimates. For example, refer to the regression equation in Table 6.5. In this model, the production cost (y) is related to the three explanatory variables: machine hours (x_1), material cost (x_2), and labor hours (x_3). If we check the effect of the variable machine hours

(x_1), the regression model indicates that for each unit increase in machine hours, the production cost (y) decreases when the other two factors are held constant. However, we would expect the production cost (y) to increase as more machine hours are used. This may be due to the presence of multicollinearity. Because of the presence of multicollinearity, the value of a β parameter may have the opposite sign from what is expected, and after the effects of x_2=material cost, and x_3 = labor hours have been accounted for. However, the result of t

One way of avoiding multicollinearity in regression is to conduct *design of experiments* and select the levels of factors in a way that the levels are uncorrelated. This may not be possible in many situations. It is not unusual to have correlated independent variables; therefore, it is important to detect the presence of multicollinearity to make the necessary modifications in the regression analysis.

Table 6.5 Regression analysis: PROD COST versus MACHINE HOURS, MATERIAL COST, and LABOR Hours

---

The regression equation is

PROD COST = − 336 − 0.897 MACHINE HOURS + 0.825 MATERIAL COST

+ 0.271 LABOR HOURS

Predictor Coef SE Coef T P VIF

Constant −335.5 159.9 −2.10 0.044

MACHINE HOURS −0.8973 0.8087 −1.11 0.276 24.239

MATERIAL COST 0.8247 0.4676 1.76 0.088 14.064

LABOR HOURS 0.2707 0.2276 1.19 0.243 10.846

S = 101.674 R-Sq = 45.6% R-Sq(adj) = 40.4%

Analysis of Variance

Source DF SS MS F P

Regression 3 269108 89703 8.68 0.000

Residual Error 31 320465 10338

Total 34 589573

Detecting Multicollinearity

Several methods are used to detect the presence of multicollinearity in regression. We will discuss two of them.

1. **Detecting Multicollinearity Using Variance Inflation Factor (VIF):**
   MINITAB provides an option to calculate VIF for each predictor variable that measures how much the variance of the estimated regression coefficients are inflated as compared to when the predictor variables are not linearly related. Use the guidelines in Table 6.6 to interpret the VIF. VIF values greater than 10 may indicate that multicollinearity is unduly influencing your regression results. In this case, you may want to reduce multicollinearity by removing unimportant independent variables from your model.
   Refer to Table 6.5 for the values of **VIF** for the production cost example. The VIF value for each predictor has a value greater than 10 indicating the presence of multicollinearity. The VIF values indicate that the predictors are highly correlated.

2. **Detecting Multicollinearity by Calculating Coefficient of Correlation, r:**
   A simple way of determining multicollinearity is to calculate the coefficient of correlation, r, between each pair of predictors or independent variables in the model. The degree of multicollinearity depends on the magnitude of the value of r. Use Table 6.7 as a guide to determine multicollinearity.

Table 6.8 shows the correlation coefficient, r *between* each pair of predictors for the production cost example.

The above values of r show that the variables are highly correlated.

Table 6.6 Detecting correlation using VIF values

Values of VIF	Predictors are…
VIF =1	Not correlated
1 < VIF < 5	Moderately correlated
VIF = 5–10 or greater	Highly correlated

Table 6.7 Determining multicollinearity using correlation coefficient, r

Correlation Coefficient, r	
$\lvert r \rvert \geq 0.8$	Extreme multicollinearity
$0.2 \leq \lvert r \rvert < 0.8$	Moderate multicollinearity
$\lvert r \rvert < 0.8$	Low multicollinearity

Table 6.8 Correlation coefficient between pairs of variables

Correlations: MACHINE HOURS, MATERIAL COST, LABOR HOURS		
MACHINE HOURS	MATERIAL COST(y)	
MATERIAL COST	0.964	
LABOR HOURS	0.953	0.917
Cell Contents: Pearson correlation		

Quadratic (Second Order) Model

The yield of a chemical process at different temperatures is shown in the Data File: **YIELD1.MTW**. The fitted line plot of the temperature and yield in Figure 6.5 indicates a nonlinear relationship. The plot shows that the data can be well approximated by a quadratic model.

(a) We used MINITAB to run a quadratic model of the form:

$$Y = w_0 + w_1 + w_2\, x^2 \ (6.10)$$

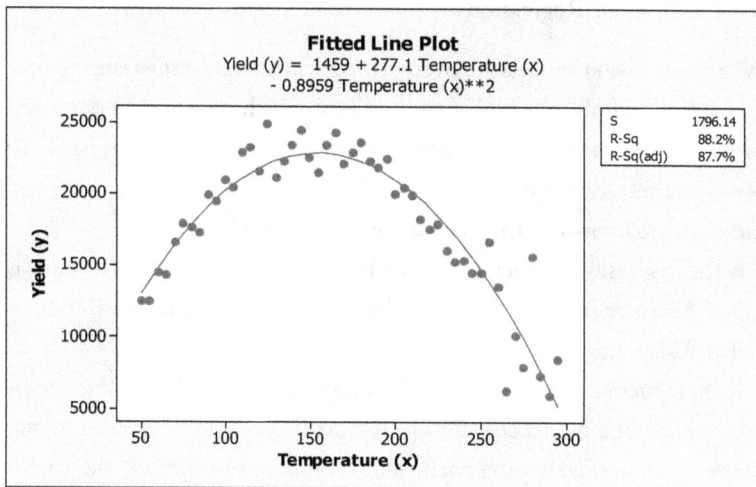

Figure 6.5 Plot showing the points and the fitted curve

The fitted quadratic model and the regression output from MINITAB are shown in Table 6.9.

(a) What is the prediction equation relating yield (y) and the temperature (x).

(b) What is the coefficient of determination? What does it tell you about the model.

The regression output from MINITAB is shown in Table 6.9.

(a) The prediction equation from the regression output in Table 14.43 is

Yield (y) = 1459 + 277 Temperature (x) - 0.896 x*x

or

$$\hat{y} = 1459 + 277x - 0.896x^2$$

(b) The coefficient of determination, R^2 is 88.2% (reported as R-Sq = 88.2%) in Table 6.9. This tells us that 88.2% of the variation in y is explained by the regression and 11.8% of the variation is unexplained or due to error.

Other Types of Regression Algorithms

Lasso and Ridge Regressions

When Regression models are overly complicated and fit the training data too well, the problem of overfitting occurs, which may lead to poor performance with new data. The problem of overfitting is a serious issue. To overcome and solve the overfitting problem, two methods are used. These methods are known as **L1 and L2 regularizations.**

The regression model that uses the L1 regularization technique is called **Lasso regression** and a model that uses the L2 regularization is called **Ridge regression.**

These methods are known as **Shrinkage** methods. Using these methods, we can fit a model containing all p predictors using a technique that *constrains* or *regularizes* the coefficient estimates, or *shrinking* the coefficient estimates toward zero. The reason behind shrinking the coefficient estimates can significantly reduce their variance. The two best-known

Table 6.9 Regression output

```
Results for: YIELD1.MTW

Regression Analysis: Yield (y) versus Temperature (x), x*x

The regression equation is
Yield (y) = 1459 + 277 Temperature (x)-0.896 x*x

Predictor              Coef  SE Coef        T      P
Constant               1459     1493     0.98  0.334
Temperature (x)      277.12    19.16    14.47  0.000
x*x                 -0.89585  0.05458  -16.41  0.000

S = 1796.14   R-Sq = 88.2%   R-Sq(adj) = 87.7%

Analysis of Variance

Source            DF          SS          MS       F      P
Regression         2  1134859671   567429836  175.89  0.000
Residual Error    47   151628370     3226136
Total             49  1286488041


Source            DF      Seq SS
Temperature (x)    1   265772263
x*x                1   869087408
```

techniques for shrinking the regression coefficients toward zero are *ridge regression* and *lasso regression.*

Lasso Regression

Lasso regression is a type of **linear regression** that uses shrinkage where data values are shrunk toward a central point, like the mean. The acronym *LASSO* stands for **least absolute shrinkage and selection operator.** This procedure creates simple, sparse models, or models with fewer parameters and is suited for regression algorithms showing high levels of multicollinearity. This is also used in cases where we want to automate certain parts of the model selection, for example, variable selection/parameter elimination.

Lasso regression uses L1 regularization that adds a penalty equal to the absolute value of the magnitude of coefficients. This type of regularization is suited for models with fewer coefficients where some coefficients can become zero and are eliminated from the model. If the penalties are larger, it may result in coefficient values closer to zero which is desirable for producing simpler models. The cost function for the Lasso regression with L1 regularization is given by:

$$\sum_{i=1}^{n} (Y_i - \beta_0 - \sum_{j=1}^{p} X_{ij} \beta_j)^2 + \lambda \sum_{j=1}^{p} |\beta_j^2| \quad (6.11)$$

where $\lambda \geq 0$ is a tuning parameter. The L1 of a coefficient vector β is given by $\sum |\beta_j|$.

Note that if lambda (λ) is zero, the model is the same as the ordinary least squares, whereas if (λ) is very large, it will make the coefficients zero leading to an underfitting situation. In the case of the lasso, the L1 penalty has the effect of forcing some of the coefficient estimates to be exactly equal to zero when the tuning parameter λ is sufficiently large.

Ridge Regression

Ridge regression is the method of analyzing multicollinearity in multiple regression data. It is used when a data set contains a large number of predictor variables. Multicollinearity is a measure of correlation among the predictors in a regression model. Multicollinearity exists when two or more independent variables in the regression model are correlated with each other. In practice, it is not unusual to see correlations among the independent variables. Serious multicollinearity may cause problems by increasing the variance of the regression coefficients making them unstable and difficult to interpret.

When the features in the model are highly linearly correlated with other features, the linear models are likely to overfit leading to model overfitting. Ridge regression uses L2 regularization that avoids overfitting by adding a penalty to models that have too large coefficients. Ridge regression is an extension of linear regression where the loss function is modified to minimize the complexity of the model. This modification is done by adding a penalty parameter that is equivalent to the square of the magnitude of the coefficients. L2 regularization, also called a ridge regression, adds the *squared magnitude* of the coefficient as the penalty term to the loss function. The loss function for this case is given by:

$$\sum_{i=1}^{n} (Y_i - \beta_0 - \sum_{j=1}^{p} X_{ij}\beta_j)^2 + \lambda \sum_{j=1}^{p} \beta_j^2 \quad (6.12)$$

where $\lambda \geq 0$ is a tuning parameter, which is determined separately. Note that if (λ) lambda is zero, the model is as same as ordinary least squares. But if (λ) lambda is very large, it adds too much weight and leads to underfitting. Therefore, choosing the right value of (λ) is important.

The key difference between L1 and L2 regularization techniques is that L1 or lasso shrinks the less important feature's coefficient to zero thus, removing some features altogether. In other words, L1 regularization works well for feature selection in case we have a huge number of features. These techniques are applied to avoid overfitting issues.

Linear Predictor Functions

The regression models discussed earlier use a **linear predictor function.** It is a linear_set of coefficients and explanatory variables (independent variables) whose value is used to predict the outcome of a dependent variable.[1*] For example, linear and multiple regression, where the coefficients are called regression coefficients.

These functions also occur in various other types of linear classifiers (e.g., logistic regression,[2*] perceptrons,[3*] support vector machines (SVMs),[4*] and linear discriminant analysis (LDA)[5*]), as well as in various other models, such as principal component analysis[6*] and factor analysis.

In many of these models, the coefficients are referred to as ***weights***. The basic form of a linear predictor function f (i) for data point *i* (consisting of *p* explanatory variables), for *i* = 1, ..., *n*, is

$$f(i) = \beta_0 + \beta_1 x_{i1} + ... + \beta_p x_{ip} \quad (2.1)$$

where x i k x_{ik}, for $k = 1, ..., p$, is the value of the kth explanatory variable for data point i, and $\beta_0, \beta_1 ..., \beta p \beta 0, ... , \beta p$ are the *coefficients* (regression coefficients, weights, etc.) indicating the relative effect of a particular *explanatory variable* on the *outcome*.

Notations

It is common to write the predictor function in a more compact form as follows:

- The coefficients $\beta_0, \beta_1, ..., \beta_p$ are grouped into a single vector β of size $p + 1$.
- For each data point i, an additional explanatory pseudo-variable x_{i0} is added, with a fixed value of 1, corresponding to the intercept coefficient β_0.
- The resulting explanatory variables $x_{i0}(= 1), x_{i1}, ..., x_{ip}$ are then grouped into a single vector x_i of size $p + 1$.

Other Supervised Learning Models

Statistical Binary Classification

Statistical classification is a supervised learning method of machine learning where the categories are predefined and are used to categorize new observations into said categories. If there are only two categories, the problem is known as statistical binary classification. Some of the methods commonly used for binary classification methods are:

- Logistic regression
- Decision trees
- Random forests
- Bayesian networks
- SVMs
- Neural networks

The binary classification techniques are classified as:

- Binary classification (logistic regression, SVM, LDA)
- Multivariate classification models (Naïve Bayes, k-nearest neighbor, random forest)

We will discuss the above machine learning algorithms for classification problems. These include logistic regression, LDA, decision trees, SVMs, random forest, k-nearest neighbor, and Naïve Bayes.

Logistic Regression

Linear regression and logistic regression are similar in some ways. In regression, the goal is to predict a target variable using one or more features or independent variables. The output of a regression model is a number or continuous variable. **Logistic regression,** on the other hand, is a **classification problem.**

Linear regression provides a continuous output, but Logistic regression has a discreet output. The simple linear regression model is given by $y = \beta_0 + \beta_1 x$. In logistic regression, we have the function of the form of linear regression, but the goal is to solve for the probability of y, $p(y)$. An example of logistic regression is whether a borrower will default on a loan. The loan granting agency would like to find the probability of a loan default based on several factors including the credit history, creditworthiness of the borrower, and so on.

Thus, in binary logistic regression, there is a single binary dependent variable, coded by an indicator variable, labeled "0" and "1," while the independent variables can each be a binary variable or a continuous variable. The probability of the value labeled "1" can vary between 0 and 1.

Suppose we would like to predict the outcome for the candidates who are required to take a standardized test. The score on the test determines whether a candidate is accepted to a university or not. The test scores and outcomes are shown in Table 6.10. Note that the outcome is binary—a "0" indicates nonacceptance, whereas a "1" indicates that the student is accepted to the university. This type of problem fits into *binary logistic regression* where the objective is to predict the probability of acceptance of a candidate based on his/her test score.

Figure 6.6 shows the plot of probability of event versus the scores. The shape of the curve in this figure is the logistic curve and is given by

$$p(x) = \frac{e^{(\beta_0 + \beta_1 x)}}{1 + e^{(\beta_0 + \beta_1 x)}} \quad (6.13)$$

where $p(x)$ denotes the probability that the candidate receiving a score x will be accepted to the university.

The computer result of this logistic regression problem is shown in Table 6.11.

The computer outputs in Table 6.11 tell us that the point estimates of β_0 and β_1 are $b_0 = -5.58$ and $b_1 = 0.01505$. These estimates in logistic regression are obtained using an advanced statistical procedure known as **maximum likelihood estimation**. Using these estimates, the probabilities for candidates who scored 390, 475, and 590 are calculated. These are shown in the computer output of Table 6.7. These probabilities are calculated using

$$\hat{p}(x) = \frac{e^{(\beta_0 + \beta_1 x)}}{1 + e^{(\beta_0 + \beta_1 x)}} = \hat{p}(590) = \frac{e^{[(-5.58+0.01505(590))]}}{1 + e^{[-5.58+0.01505(590)]}} = 0.964259$$

Thus, $\hat{p}(590) = 0.964259$ is the point estimate of the probability that a candidate scoring 590 on the standardized test has 0.9643 percent chance of being accepted to the university. The MINITAB output in Table 6.7 also gives the probability, $\hat{p}(x)$ for $x = 390$ and $x = 475$. Figure 6.6 shows the plot of estimated probabilities, and the dashed bands around the curve are confidence intervals for the true probabilities. The general logistic regression model can be extended to k independent variables. The probability that an event (such as the score on the standardized test) will occur to k independent variables $x_1, x_2, ..., x_k$ is

$$\hat{p}(x_1, x_2, ..., x_k) = \frac{e^{(\beta_0 + \beta_1 x_1 + \beta_2 x_2 + ... + \beta_k x_k)}}{1 + e^{(\beta_0 + \beta_1 x_1 + \beta_2 x_2 + ... + \beta_k x_k)}} \quad (6.14)$$

where $p(x_1, x_2, ..., x_k)$ is the probability that the event will occur when the values of the independent variables are $x_1, x_2, ..., x_k$. The coefficients $\beta_0, \beta_1, \beta_2 ..., \beta_1$ are obtained from n observations or the data points. Here,

Table 6.10 Data for logistic regression

Data

1

Outcome	0	0	0	0	0	0	1	0	1	0	1	0	1	0	1	1
Score	150	175	200	225	250	275	275	300	325	350	375	400	425	450	500	525

2

Outcome	1	1	1	1
Score	550	575	600	650

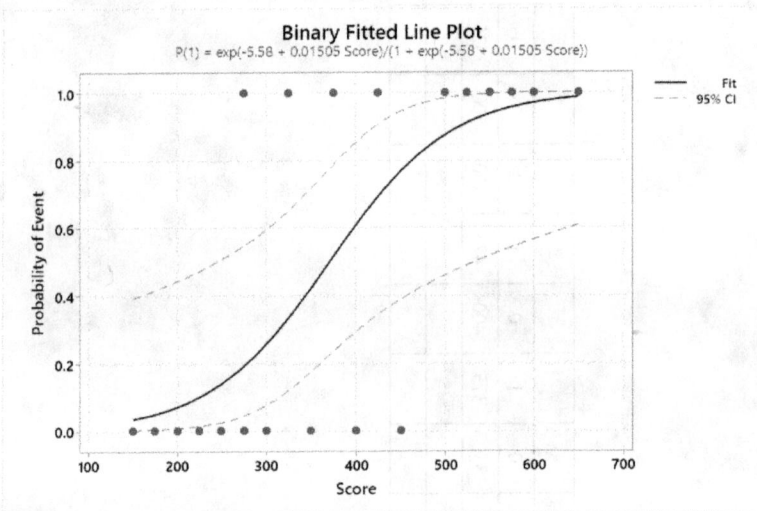

Figure 6.6 Binary fitted line plot

y (or, the outcome in our example) is a dummy variable that is equal to 1 if the event occurs or 0 otherwise.

In logistic regression, the odds of success are often calculated using the probability of success of an independent variable, x. For example, the odds of success for a potential student applying for acceptance to the university is defined to be the probability of success divided by the probability of failure for the student. That is,

$$Odds = \frac{\text{probability of success}}{\text{probability of failure}} = \frac{p(x)}{1 - p(x)} \quad (6.15)$$

For a student who scored 590 on the standardized test, the probability of success calculated was 0.9643. (See the computer output in Table 6.11). Therefore, we estimate the odds of success are:

$$Odds = \frac{p(x)}{1 - p(x)} = \frac{p(570)}{1 - p(570)} = \frac{0.9643}{1 - 0.9643} = 27.01$$

Thus, the odds of success for the student are 27 to 1.

Table 6.11 MINITAB *computer output for standardized test*

LOGISTICREG (EXAMPLE)

Binary Logistic Regression: Outcome versus Score

Method

Link function	Logit
Rows used	20

Response Information

Variable	Value	Count	
Outcome	1	10	(Event)
	0	10	
	Total	20	

Regression Equation

P(1)	=	exp(Y')/(1 + exp(Y'))
Y'	=	−5.58 + 0.01505 score

Continued...

Coefficients

Term	Coef	SE Coef	95% CI	Z-Value	P-Value	VIF
Constant	−5.58	2.36	(−10.21, −0.96)	−2.37	0.018	
Score	0.01505	0.00629	(0.00272, 0.02737)	2.39	0.017	1.00

Odds Ratios for Continuous Predictors

	Odds Ratio	95% CI
Score	1.0152	(1.0027, 1.0277)

Model Summary

Deviance R-Sq	Deviance R-Sq(adj)	AIC	AICc	BIC	Area Under ROC Curve
42.08%	38.47%	20.06	20.77	22.05	0.8950

Goodness-of-Fit Tests

Test	DF	Chi-Square	P-Value
Deviance	18	16.06	0.588
Pearson	18	14.60	0.689
Hosmer–Lemeshow	8	3.07	0.930

(continued)

Table 6.11 (Continued)

Settings

Variable	Setting
Score	390

Prediction

Fitted Probability	SE Fit	95% CI
0.570957	0.159766	(0.270412, 0.826934)

Settings

Variable	Setting
Score	475

Prediction

Fitted Probability	SE Fit	95% CI
0.827028	0.135793	(0.426587, 0.968483)

Continued...

Settings

Variable	Setting
Score	590

Prediction

Fitted Probability	SE Fit	95% CI
0.964259	0.0539869	(0.555968, 0.998283)

Linear Discriminant Analysis (LDA)

1. LDA is a supervised learning algorithm used for classification tasks
   in machine learning. This method is used to classify observations
   into two or more groups when a sample with known groups is available. This method is used to (a) determine how accurately the observations are classified into the known groups, (b) determine how the
   predictor variables differentiate the groups, and (c) make predictions
   for the groups for new observations for unknown groups. LDA is
   a dimensionality reduction technique used for supervised classification problems. It is used for modeling and separating two or more

classes. It projects the features in higher dimension space into a lower dimension space. The classes to be separated can have multiple features. Using only a single feature to classify them may result in some overlapping.

2. LDA is used to find a linear combination of features that best separates the classes in a data set.

3. The method works by projecting the data onto a lower-dimensional space. This maximizes the separation between the classes by finding a set of linear discriminants that maximize the ratio between-class variance to within-class variance.

4. LDA is based on the assumption that the data has a Gaussian distribution and that the covariance matrices of the different classes are equal. The other assumption is that the data are linearly separable so that a linear decision boundary can accurately classify the different classes.

LDA is computationally efficient and works well with the data having many features. The algorithm can also handle multicollinearity in the data. Usually, the classes can have multiple features. Using only a single feature to classify them may result in some overlapping.

The **limitations** of this method are the violations of some of the assumptions. The assumptions that the data are linearly separable, the data follow a normal distribution, and the covariance matrices of different classes are equal may not hold.

Example

Suppose we have two sets of data points with two different classes that we need to classify. Figure 6.7 shows the data points plotted on a 2D plane. It can be clearly seen that there is not a unique straight line that can completely separate the data points of the two classes. In such cases, LDA is used that reduces the 2D graph into a 1D graph in order to maximize the separability between the two classes.

Here, LDA uses both axes (X and Y) to create a new axis and projects data onto a new axis in a way to maximize the separation of the two

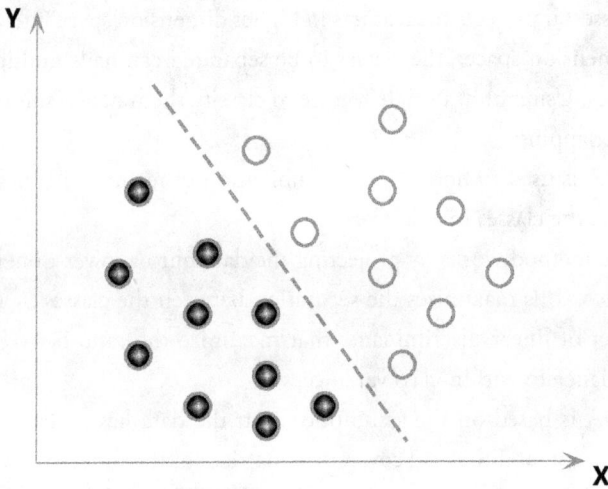

Figure 6.7 Two sets of data points with two classes

categories reducing the 2D graph into a 1D graph . Two criteria are used by LDA to create a new axis:

1. Maximize the distance between the means of the two classes.
2. Minimize the variation within each class.

In Figure 6.8, a new axis shown as the dashed line is generated and plotted in the 2D graph. This maximizes the distance between the means of the two classes and minimizes the variation within each class. This newly generated axis increases the separation between the data points of two. After creating the new axis, all the data points of the two classes are plotted on a new axis as shown in Figure 6.9.

Note: The linear discriminant analysis fails when the mean of the distributions is different. In such cases, it becomes impossible for LDA to find the axis that separates both classes linearly. The solution then is to use nonlinear discriminant analysis. The mathematical treatment of LDA can be found in several literature.

Support Vector Machine (SVM)

A SVM is a supervised machine learning algorithm that is used to divide the data set into two classes. The method can be applied for both

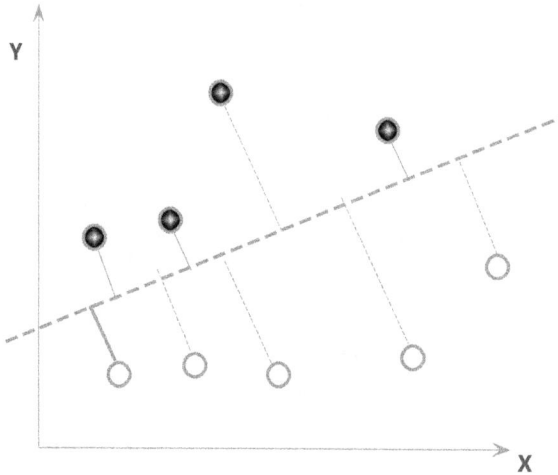

Figure 6.8 New axis maximizing the distance between the means

classification and regression problems but is commonly used for classification problems. Here we discuss the SVM approach applied to classification problems. The main idea behind SVM is to determine a hyperplane that best divides the data set into two classes. Figure 6.10 shows a hyperplane separating two sets of data. One set is shown as dark points and the other with open circles with no fill color.

What Are Support Vectors?

Support vectors are the data points nearest to the hyperplane (see Figure 6.10). These points are critical elements of the set. Removing these points would alter the position of the hyperplane.

What Is a Hyperplane?

For a classification problem with only two features as in Figure 6.10, a hyperplane can be thought of as a line that linearly separates the data set and classifies them. For the hyperplane to correctly classify the data sets, the distance between the hyperplane and the data points should be as further apart as possible, that is, the data points should be as far from the hyperplane as possible while still on the correct side of the hyperplane.

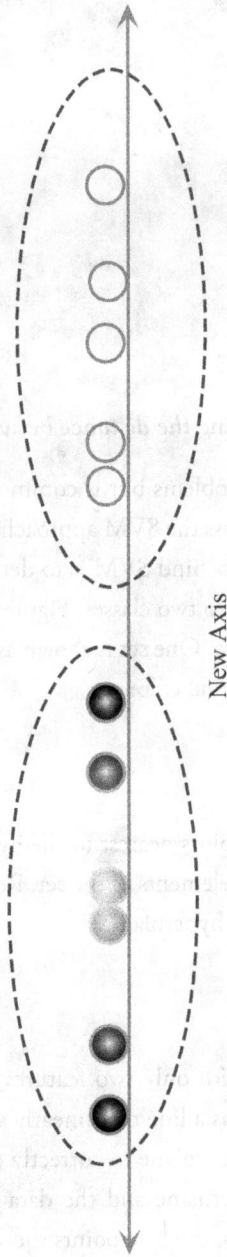

Figure 6.9 Data points on a new axis

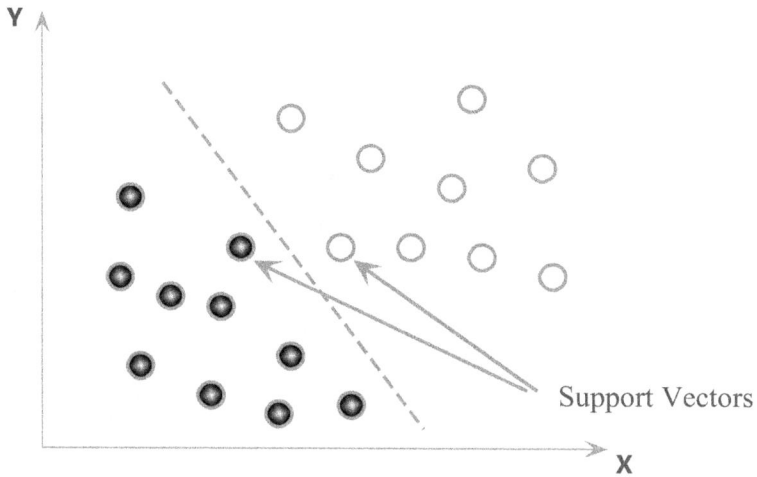

Figure 6.10 Hyperplane separating two sets of data

For the new data set, the correct class is determined based on the side of the hyperplane the data lands.

Finding the Right Hyperplane

The hyperplane should be selected in a way so it best segregates the two classes in a data set. The hyperplane is selected based on the largest possible margin (the distance between the hyperplane and the nearest data point from either set is known as the margin) between the hyperplane and any point within the data set. This provides a higher chance of new data being classified correctly. Figure 6.11 shows the concept of margin.

It is not always possible to determine a unique hyperplane that classifies the two sets of data as the data are rarely clean enough so that a well-defined hyperplane is defined. The data sets are usually jumbled or mixed, which makes it difficult to separate the data set linearly. Figure 6.12 shows a case where it is not possible to clearly separate the two sets linearly, that is, there is no clear hyperplane. One possible solution in such cases is to project the data in 3D view.

This can be explained using another example. Suppose that the two sets of data (represented by solid and blank circles) are on a sheet and the sheet is lifted launching the points in the air. While the data points represented by balls are in the air, the sheet can be used to separate them.

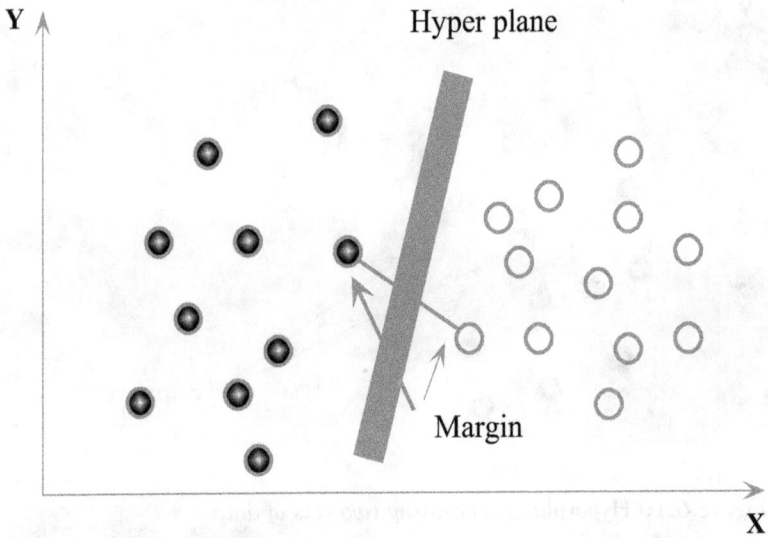

Figure 6.11 Hyperplane and margin

This lifting is mapping the data into a higher dimension and the process is known as **Kernelling***. The process is explained in Figure 6.13. This leads

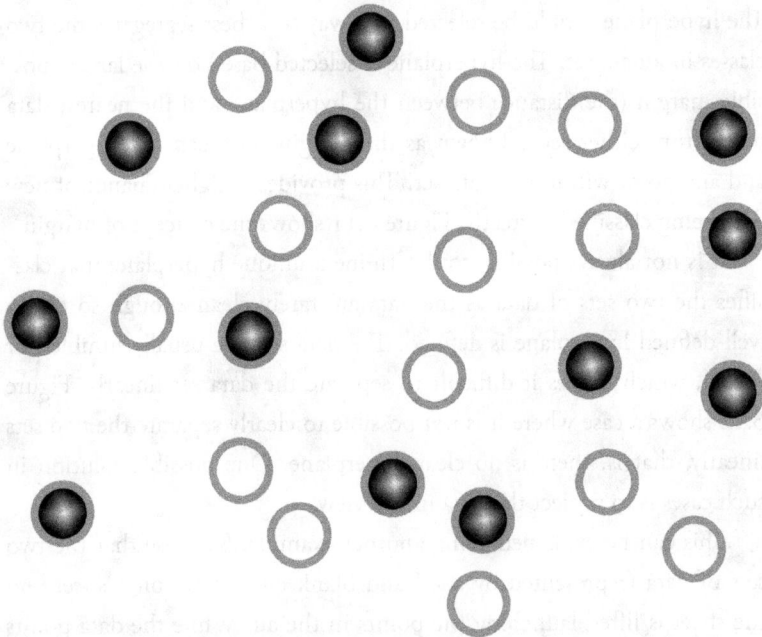

Figure 6.12 Data sets with no clear hyperplane

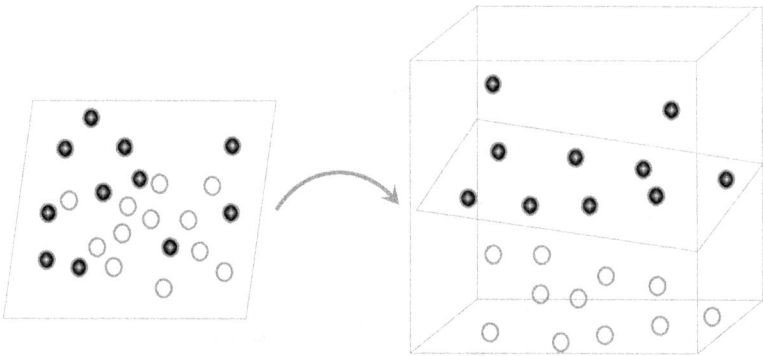

Figure 6.13 Separating classes with a plane

to a hyperplane that is not linear but a plane. The data are thus continued to be mapped in higher dimensions until a hyperplane is found that segregates the data and is classified in the right group.

Kernelling: In SVM algorithms, kernels are a set of mathematical functions that are defined as the kernel. The function of the kernel is to take the data as input and transform it into the required form. Different SVM algorithms use different types of kernel functions. These functions can be of different types. These functions can be *linear, nonlinear, polynomial, radial basis function, and sigmoid.*

Thus, in a 2D example, we have some data points on a grid that we want to separate by the category they should fit in without having the data in the wrong category. This leads to finding a line between the two data sets using the closest points in the sets that keep the other data points separated. The two closest data points give us the support vectors used to find the line. That line is called the *decision boundary*. The decision boundary does not have to be only a line. It can also be a hyperplane as the decision boundary can be found using any number of features, not just two. It can also be nonlinear. Figure 6.14 shows an example of a nonlinear SVM.

The nonlinear SVM uses the kernelling method which provides more flexibility as it can add more features to fit a hyperplane compared to a two-dimensional space. The simple SVM, on the other hand, is used for linear regression and classification problems.

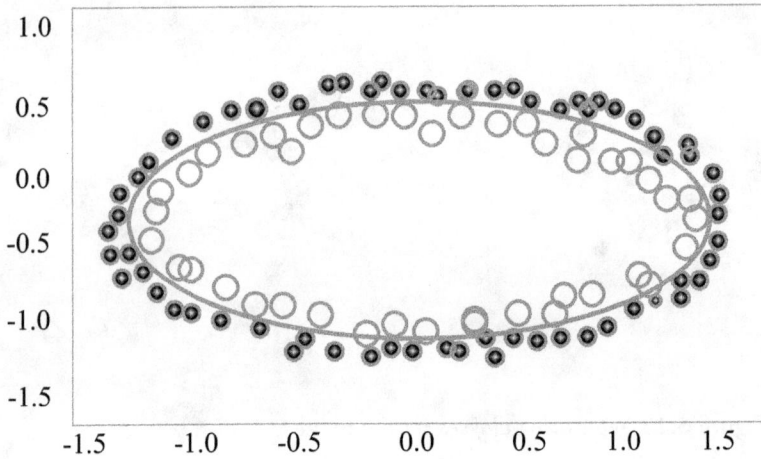

Figure 6.14 A nonlinear SVM

Applications

SVMs have applications in email classification, gene classification, hand-writing recognition, face detection, web applications, and more. It can handle both classification and regression on linear and nonlinear data.

SVMs can find complex relationships between the data without going through a lot of transformations. It is efficient with smaller data sets. SVMs in general have better accuracy compared to other methods. The method is effective in cases where number of features is greater than the number of data points.

SVM applications are in text classification tasks, detecting spam and sentiment analysis, and image recognition challenges. It performs well in aspect-based recognition and color-based classification. It also has applications in many areas of handwritten digit recognition, such as postal automation services.

Related Topics:

- How to Select Support Vector Machine Kernels? (www. kdnuggets.com/2016/06/select-support-vector-machine-kernels.html)
- When Does Deep Learning Work Better Than SVMs or Random Forests? (www.kdnuggets.com/2016/04/deep-learning-vs-svm-random-forest.html)

Classification and Regression Trees (CART)

CART are **predictive algorithms or predictive analytics models used in machine learning**. These are used to predict the target variable, which is a quantitative response variable, for example, weekly demand for a company, utility consumption, water consumption by families, or sales, we use the decision trees known as **regression trees**. If the target or response variable is qualitative or categorical, for example, whether a consumer with a purchase of a specific amount will redeem a coupon for the next purchase, we use a **classification tree**. CART can be implemented using the classification and regression algorithm in **Scikit-Learn** to train decision trees.

Data Considerations for CART Classification

To make sure that the results are valid, the following guidelines are helpful in data collection, analysis, and interpretation of the results. The response variable should be categorical for classification problems. Categorical variables contain a finite, countable number of categories or distinct groups. Categorical data may or may not have a logical order. For example, categorical variables include gender, material type, payment method, a *Yes* or *No* response. If the response variable has two categories, such as pass or fail, then the response is binary. If the response variable contains three or more categories, then the response is multinomial. The data for the response variable must be either text values or numeric values.

If the response variable is continuous, CART Regression is used. Predictor variables may be continuous or categorical. A combination of continuous or categorical predictors can be used. A test set is recommended when the number of cases is greater than 500.

It is suggested to use cross-validation when the number of cases is ≤5,000. In cases where the number of cases is larger than 5,000, a test set is recommended. For a large set of data, validation with a training set and a test set of data should be used.

The CART Classification model is used to create a decision tree for a binomial or multinomial categorical response with many categorical and continuous predictor variables. This Classification model can identify important patterns and relationships between a categorical response and predictors even within highly complicated data, without using parametric methods.

CART Classification models have a wide range of applications, including fraud detection, credit rating, manufacturing, quality control, predicting customer response rates, and others. (For a more complete introduction to the CART methodology, see Breiman, Friedman, Olshen and Stone (1984)[1].)

Types of Classification Algorithms

Different types of classification algorithms have been developed over time and are in use. The algorithms are designed to provide the best results for classification tasks by employing techniques like bagging and boosting. Among the widely used classification algorithms are:

- Decision tree
- Random forest classifier
- K-nearest neighbors
- SVM

Decision Trees

A decision tree is one of the most powerful and widely used tools of supervised learning. It is a tree structure consisting of nodes and branches. In the decision tree, the nodes are split into subnodes based on a threshold value of an attribute. The root node is taken as the training set and is split into two by considering the best attribute and threshold value. It is constructed by recursively splitting the training data into subsets based on the values of the attributes until a stopping criterion is met, such as the maximum depth of the tree or the minimum number of samples required to split a node.

During training, the decision tree algorithm selects the best attribute to split the data based on a metric known as *entropy* or ***Gini impurity***. These measure the level of impurity or randomness in the subsets. The goal is to find the attribute that maximizes the information gain or reduces or minimizes the impurity after the split.

Decision tree is used for both classification and regression problems. It is also used in *random forest* to train different subsets of training data. The random forest is one of the most powerful algorithms in machine learning.

Common Terms and Their Meaning in Decision Tree

Some common Terminologies used in Decision Trees (refer to Figure 6.15):

- **Root node:** it is the topmost node in the tree. It represents the complete data set and is the starting point of the decision-making process.
- **Decision/internal node:** a node that denotes a choice regarding an input feature. Branching of internal nodes leads to the leaf nodes or other internal nodes.
- **Leaf/terminal node:** a node without any child nodes. It indicates a class label or a numerical value.
- **Splitting:** is the process of splitting a node into two or more subnodes using a split criterion using a selected feature.
- **Branch/subtree:** a subsection of the decision tree starts at an internal node or decision node and ends at the leaf nodes.
- **Parent node:** the node that is divided into one or more child nodes.
- **Child node:** the nodes emerging from splitting a parent node.
- **Impurity:** impurity is a measurement of the target variable's homogeneity in a subset of data.
- Impurity refers to the degree of randomness or uncertainty in a set of examples. The two matrices—Gini **index** and **entropy**, are two commonly used impurity measurements in decision trees for classification purposes.
- **Variance:** the variance is a measure of variation between the predicted and the target variables. Variance measures how much the predicted and the target variables vary in different samples of a data set. This is used in regression problems in decision trees. The common matrices for regression are **mean**

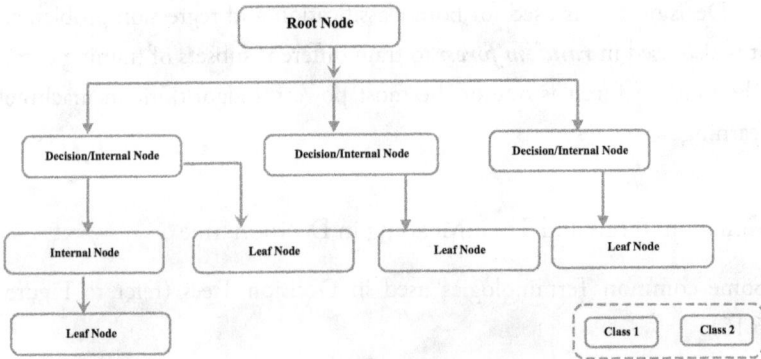

Figure 6.15 A general structure decision tree

> **squared error, mean absolute error, Friedman_mse, or half Poisson deviance.** These are commonly used to measure the variance for the regression in the decision tree.
> - **Information gain:** it is a measure of the reduction in impurity achieved by splitting a data set on a particular feature in a decision tree.
> - The splitting criterion is using the feature that offers the greatest information gain.
> - **Pruning:** the process of removing branches from the tree that are redundant or do not provide any information or lead to overfitting.

Figure 6.15 shows the general structure of the decision tree.

CART algorithm uses **Gini impurity** to split the data set into a decision tree by searching for the best homogeneity for the subnodes using the Gini index criterion.

Gini Impurity

Gini impurity is a metric that evaluates the accuracy of a split among the classified groups. It is an evaluation metric used to evaluate the decision tree model. It stores the sum of the squared probabilities of each class. It computes the degree of probability of a specific variable that is wrongly being classified. Its value is between 0 and 1. A value of 0 means all observations belong to one class and a 1 indicates a random distribution of the elements within the classes. A value of 0.5 is an indication that the elements are uniformly distributed into classes. The desirable value of the Gini index is close to 1.

The Gini impurity is calculated as:

$$Gini = 1 - \sum_{i=1}^{n}(p_i)^2 \quad (6.16)$$

where p_1 is the probability of an object being classified in a particular class.

It works on categorical variables, provides outcomes of either *success* or *failure*, and hence conducts binary splitting only.

Entropy

Entropy measures the degree of randomness or uncertainty in the data set. In the case of classifications, it measures randomness based on the distribution of class labels in the data set.

The entropy of 0 is an indication that the data set being completely homogeneous. It means that each instance belongs to the same class with no uncertainty in the data set. When the entropy is at the highest level, it is an indication of maximum uncertainty in the data set. Entropy is a metric used to evaluate the quality of a split. The helps to select the attribute that minimizes the entropy of the resulting subsets. This does that by splitting the data set into more homogeneous subsets.

CART models are formed by selecting input variables and evaluating split points on those variables until an appropriate tree is produced.

> **Greedy algorithm**: in this case, the input space is divided using the Greedy method, which is also known as recursive binary spitting. In this method, all of the values are aligned, and several other split points are tried and assessed using a cost function.
> **Stopping criterion**: as it works, it is way down the tree, the recursive binary splitting must know when to stop splitting. The most frequent halting method is to use a minimum amount of training data allocated to every leaf node. If the count is smaller than the specified

threshold, the split is halted and the node is considered the last leaf node.

Tree pruning: decision tree's complexity is defined as the number of splits in the tree. Trees with fewer branches are recommended as they are simple to grasp and less prone to cluster the data. Working through each leaf node in the tree and evaluating the effect of deleting it using a hold-out test set is the quickest and simplest pruning approach.

Advantages of CART

- It is simple to understand. The logic is like human decision making.
- It is very useful in nonparametric and nonlinear models of classification and regression.
- CART are capable of implicitly performing feature selection.
- They are not affected by outliers. Outliers have no meaningful effect on CART.

Limitations of CART

- May result in overfitting.
- May result in high variance and low bias.

Applications of CART

- Classification algorithms are useful models for categorical data.
- Has applications in finance, blood donor classification, and others.

Difference Between Classification and Regression Tree

A classification tree is an algorithm where the target variable is categorical. The algorithm is then used to identify the *class* within which the target variable is most likely to fall. Classification trees are used when the data set needs to be split into classes that belong to the response variable (like yes or no).

Regression Tree

A Regression tree is an algorithm where the target variable is continuous, and the tree is used to predict its value. Regression trees are used when the response variable is continuous. For example, if the response variable is the temperature of the day.

Random Forest Classifier

Random forest is a supervised machine learning algorithm. In the case of classification, it is made of decision trees. It combines **the output of multiple decision trees to reach a single result**. The number of trees may range from 50 **to 400 trees**. Its ease of use and flexibility have made it popular. It is used for both classification and regression problems and is based on *ensemble learning*, which **integrates multiple classifiers**. Ensemble learning methods are a set of classifiers, for example, decision trees. The predictions from the decision trees are combined to identify the single most popular result. The most well-known ensemble methods are ***bagging*** or bootstrap aggregation and ***boosting***.

The bagging method was introduced by Leo Breiman in 1996. In 1996, the method used a random sample of data in a training set. The sample is selected with replacement so that the individual data points can be selected more than once. After several samples are generated, the models are trained independently. Depending upon whether the problem is that of classification or regression, the average of the predictions is considered and usually yields a more accurate result. This approach is used to reduce the variance in a noisy data set.

The random forest algorithm is an extension of the bagging method. It uses both bagging and feature randomness to create a forest of decision trees that are uncorrelated. Feature randomness or feature bagging generates a random subset of features with low correlation among the decision trees. The main difference between the decision trees and random forests

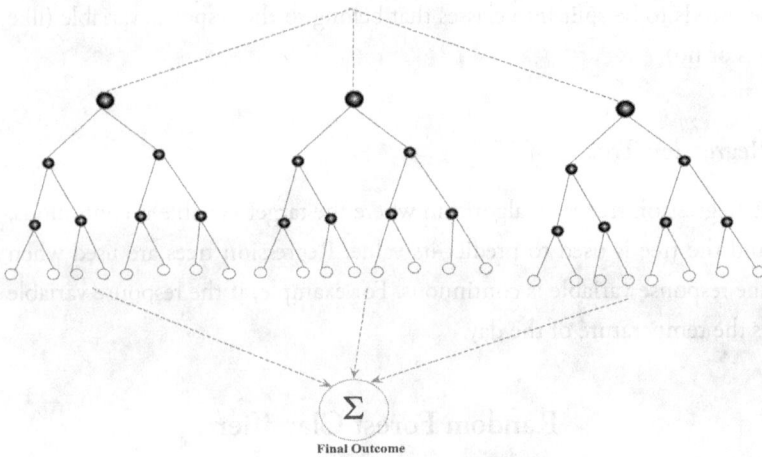

Figure 6.16 Combining the outcome of several trees

is that the decision trees consider all possible feature splits, while random forests use a subset of features.

Random forest algorithms have three main hyperparameters that need to be set before training. These are node size, the number of trees, and the number of features to be sampled. With this, the random forest classifier can be used for regression or classification problems.

As mentioned earlier, the random forest algorithm is made up of a collection of decision trees. Each tree in the ensemble consists of a data sample drawn from a training set with a replacement known as a bootstrap sample. Out of that training sample one-third of it is set aside as test data. Depending on the type of problem—classification or regression the result of the prediction will vary. In the regression problem, the individual decision trees are averaged. For a classification task, the most frequent categorical variable is selected as the predicted class (Figure 6.16).

Naïve Bayes Classifier

The Naïve Bayes classifier is a supervised machine learning algorithm, which is used for classification tasks like text classification. It is also part of a family of generative learning algorithms meaning that it seeks to model the distribution of inputs of a given class or category.

The Naïve Bayes classifier works **on the principle of conditional probability, as given by the Bayes theorem**, used in a wide variety of classification tasks.

While calculating the math on probability, we usually denote the probability of an event A as P(A). For example, the probability of getting two heads in a toss of two coins, P(2H) = 1/4.

Bayes Theorem

Bayes' theorem has application in calculating conditional probability. It uses a simple mathematical expression for this purpose.

Conditional probability is a measure of the probability of an event given that another event has already occurred. The occurred event can be determined by assumption, presumption, assertion, or evidence. The conditional probability is written as $P(A|B)$, which is read as the probability of an event A given that event B has already occurred or simply the probability of an event A given B. The formula for Bayes' theorem is written as:

$$P(A|B) = \frac{P(B|A) \cdot P(A)}{P(B)} \quad (6.17)$$

In the above equation, $P(A|B)$ is the probability of an event A given that event B has already occurred, $P(A|B)$ is the probability of an event B given that event A has already occurred, $P(A)$ and $P(B)$ are the simple probabilities of events A and B. $P(A|B)$ is also known as posterior probability, when we know: how often B happens *given that A happens*, written $P(A|B)$, how likely A is on its own, written $P(A)$, and how likely B is on its own, written $P(B)$, which are the probabilities of events A and B. Bayes' theorem is a way of finding a probability when we know certain other probabilities.

Assumptions of Naïve Bayes

The fundamental Naïve Bayes assumption is that each feature is independent and has an equal contribution.

Example: The following example demonstrates the working of this algorithm.

Suppose you are trying to decide whether to go on a hike. The decision to go hiking will be based on the weather condition. We are interested in predicting the chance or probability that the decision to hike is a *Yes* or *No*. given the weather condition on a certain day. Table 6.12 shows the data and the decisions made based on the weather conditions. Four attributes or features are considered. These are weather condition (clear, cloudy, or rainy), outside temperature (hot, moderate, or cold), humidity (high or low), and wind condition (weak or strong). The data are shown in Table 6.8. The last column in the table shows the decision which is the target value (***Yes*** or ***No***).

Assumptions: (1) The features are **independent** of each other. (2) Each feature has the same importance and influence in the prediction of the target (y) and they contribute equally.

In our data set above, **the decision to go hiking is *Yes* or *No*, given the features in Table 6.12**. Note that the columns represent the features, and the rows represent individual entries. If we take the first row of the data set, we can see that the decision to go on a hike is *NO* when the weather condition is clear, outside temperature is hot, humidity is high, and wind is weak. Based on a new instance, we would like to use **Naïve Bayes algorithm** to make a prediction for a new instance.

Suppose the new instance is **Weather Condition = Clear, Outside Temperature is Cold, Humidity = High**, and **Wind = Strong**.

For this new instance or given conditions, we would like to predict whether to go on a hike is *Yes* or *No*.

According to this example, Bayes theorem can be rewritten as:

$$P(y\Big|X) = \frac{P(X|y)P(y)}{P(X)} \quad (6.18)$$

Table 6.12 Data for Naïve Bayes algorithm

Weather Condition	Outside Temperature	Humidity	Wind	Go Hiking (Y/N)
Clear	Hot	High	Weak	N
Clear	Hot	High	Strong	N
Cloudy	Hot	High	Weak	Y
Rainy	Moderate	High	Weak	Y
Rainy	Cold	Low	Weak	Y
Rainy	Cold	Low	Strong	N
Cloudy	Cold	Low	Strong	Y
Clear	Moderate	High	Weak	N
Clear	Cold	Low	Weak	Y
Rainy	Moderate	Low	Weak	Y
clear	Moderate	Low	Strong	Y
Cloudy	Moderate	High	Strong	Y
Cloudy	Hot	Low	Weak	Y
Rainy	Moderate	High	Strong	N
Rainy	Cold	High	Weak	N

where y is the target variable that represents whether to go on a hike (Y or N) given the conditions; X represents the features:

$$X = (x_1, x_2, x_3, ..., x_n)$$

where $x_1, x_2, x_3, ..., x_n$ are the features. By substituting for **X**—the features—and expanding using the chain rule, we get:

$$P(y|x_1, x_2, ..., x_n) = \frac{P(x_1|y) \cdot P(x_2|y) \cdot P(x_3|y).....P(x_n|y) \cdot P(y)}{P(x_1) \cdot P(x_2)......P(x_n)} \quad (6.19)$$

The values for each probability can be obtained from the given data in Table 6.12. Substituting the values in the above equation will give the required probability in the above formula. For all entries in the data set, the denominator in the equation does not change, it remains static. Therefore, the denominator can be removed, and proportionality can be used. The equation can be written as:

$$P(y|x_1, x_2 ...., x_n) \propto P(y) \prod_{i-1}^{n} P(x_i|y) \quad (6.20)$$

In our example, the class/target variable (**y**) has only two outcomes, **yes** or **no**. In other cases, the classification could be multivariate. In such cases, we need to find the class variable (**y**) with the maximum probability given by

$$y = \text{argmax}_y P(y) \prod_{i-1}^{n} P(x_i \mid y) \quad (6.21)$$

Using the above function, we can obtain the class or the target, given the predictors/features in the data.

The posterior probability $P(y|X)$ can be calculated by creating a **frequency table** for each attribute or feature against the target. Then, molding the frequency tables into **likelihood tables** and using the Naïve Bayesian equation to calculate the posterior probability for each class. The class with the highest posterior probability is the outcome of the prediction. The frequency and likelihood tables for all three predictors along with the calculations are shown below.

We want to classify the new instance into a Yes (**Y**) or No (**N**) category where a Y indicates Go on a hike and N indicates otherwise. The new instance is:

Weather Condition = Clear, Outside Temperature = Cold, Humidity = High, and **Wind = Strong**

Using the data in Table 6.12, we first calculate the prior and conditional (or posterior) probabilities.

1. Calculate the **prior probabilities** that are the probabilities of Yes (Y) and No (N). From the last column of Table 6.8.

$$P(\textit{Go hiking} = \textit{yes}) = 9 / 15 = 0.60\theta$$
$$P(\textit{Go hiking} = \textit{no}) = 6 / 15 = 0.40$$

2. Calculate the **conditional probabilities or current probabilities** of individual attributes. There are four attributes or features—weather condition, outside temperature, humidity, and wind. The conditional probabilities of each are shown below.

Weather Condition	Possible	Outcomes
	Y	N
Clear	P(Clear | Y) = 2/9	P(Clear | N) = 3/6
Cloudy	P(Cloudy | Y) = 4/9	P(Cloudy | N) = 0
Rainy	P(Rainy | Y) = 3/9	P(Rainy | N) = 3/6

Outside Temp.	Possible	Outcomes
	Y	N
Hot	P(Hot | Y) = 2/9	P(Hot | N) = 2/6
Moderate	P(Moderate | Y) = 4/9	P(Moderate | N) = 2/6
Cold	P(Cloud | Y) = 3/9	P(Cloud | N) = 2/6

Humidity	Possible	Outcomes
	Y	N
High	P(High | Y) = 3/9	P(High | N) = 5/6
Low	P(Low | Y) = 6/9	P(Low | N) = 1/6

Wind	Possible	Outcomes
	Y	N
Strong	P(Strong | Y) = 3/9	P(Strong | N) = 3/6
Weak	P(Weak | Y) = 6/9	P(Weak | N) = 2/6

Based on the above probabilities, we can use the Naïve Bayes classifier equation to classify the new instance or condition to classify the new instance into Yes (Y) or No (N). The new instance for classification is

Weather Condition = Clear, Temperature + Cold, Humidity = High, Wind = Strong

We need to find out whether this new condition belongs to **Y or N**. The Naïve Bayes classifier equation is given by:

$$v_{NB} = \underset{v_j \in [Yes, No]}{\operatorname{argmax}} P(y) \prod_{i-1}^{n} P(a_i | v_j) \quad (6.22)$$

Yes and No are two targets, a_i are the given set of attributes or features, v_j is the possible outcomes (Yes or No)

$$v_{NB}(Yes) = \underset{v_j \in [Yes, No]}{\operatorname{argmax}} P(v_j) * P(\text{Weather cond.} = \text{Clear} | v_j)$$

$$P(\text{Temperature} = \text{Cold} | v_j) P(\text{Humidity} = \text{High} | v_j) P(\text{Wind} = \text{Strong} | v_j)$$

Replacing v_j first by (Yes) and then with (No) in the above equation, we calculate the probabilities shown below.

v_{NB}(Yes) = P(Yes) * P(Weather cond. = Clear$|Yes$) P(Temperature = Cold$|Yes$)

P(Humidity = High$|Yes$)P(Wind = Strong$|Yes$)

$$= \left(\frac{9}{15}\right) . \frac{2}{9} . \frac{3}{9} . \frac{3}{9} . \frac{3}{9} = 0.1777$$

v_{NB}(No) = P(No) * P(Weather cond. = Clear$|No$)P(Temperature = Cold$|No$)

P(Humidity = High$|No$)P(Wind = Strong$|No$)

$$= \left(\frac{6}{15}\right) . \frac{3}{6} . \frac{2}{6} . \frac{5}{6} . \frac{3}{6} = 0.0277$$

Normalizing these probabilities:

$$v_{NB}(Yes) = \frac{v_{NB}(Yes)}{v_{NB}(Yes) + v_{NB}(No)} = \frac{0.1777}{0.1777 + 0.0277} = 0.8651$$

$$v_{NB}(No) = \frac{v_{NB}(No)}{v_{NB}(Yes) + v_{NB}(No)} = \frac{0.0277}{0.1777 + 0.0277} = 0.1348$$

This shows that the probability of *Yes* is greater than the probability of *No*. Therefore, the new instance should be classified as *Yes* meaning that the person will decide to go on a hike.

The other classification algorithm discussed next is K-nearest neighbors.

K-Nearest Neighbors

The K-nearest neighbors algorithm (also known as KNN or K-NN) is **a nonparametric, supervised learning classifier** that uses proximity to make classifications or predictions about the grouping of an individual data point.

This algorithm is used for both regression and classification problems but is commonly used for classification. The algorithm assumes that similar points can be found near one another or similar points exist in proximity.

In **K-nearest neighbors classification**, data points are classified based on their k-closest neighbors. **K-nearest neighbors regression** predicts continuous values by averaging the outputs of the k-closest neighbors.

K-nearest neighbors algorithm has applications in different branches including finance (default on a loan), health care (classifying whether a patient has a certain disease), image and video patterns, classifying a voter, and so on.

K-Nearest Neighbors Algorithm

- **In K-nearest neighbors classification**, data points are classified based on their k-closest neighbors. It assumes the similarity between the new case or data and available cases and puts the new data or case into the category that is most similar to the other available categories.
- K-NN algorithm stores all the available data and classifies a new data point based on the similarity. This means when new data appears, it is classified into an appropriate category by using K-NN algorithm. The algorithm is explained later in this section.
- K-NN algorithm can be used to solve both regression and classification problems but its application is more common in classification problems.
- K-NN algorithm is not based on any assumption regarding the distribution of underlying data. It is a **nonparametric algorithm**.
- It is considered a **lazy learner algorithm** as it does not learn from the training set. It stores the data set and at the time of classification, it performs an action on the data set.
- K-NN algorithm at the training phase just stores the data set and when it gets new data, then it classifies that data into a category that is similar to the new data.
- **Example:** suppose we have an image of creatures that look similar to cats and dogs. We would like to classify the animals to the correct category—a cat or a dog—based on the several images provided. For this identification, we can use the KNN

algorithm, as it works on a similarity measure. Our KNN model will find the similar features of the new data set of the cats and dogs' images provided, based on the most similar features it will put it in either the cat or dog category.

How Does the K-Nearest Neighbors Algorithm Work?

Given two groups or classes or data (categories A and B). Suppose a new data point is introduced with the purpose to classify the data in the correct category. The K-NN algorithms can be used for this purpose. This algorithm compares the new data entry to the values in a given data set with different classes or categories using a distance or proximity measure. The process can be broken down into the following steps:

Another Example of Steps

- **Step 1:** suppose there are two classes or categories (Categories A and B) denoted by different data points as shown in Figure 6.17. Suppose a new data point or class is introduced. The problem is to classify the new case into the correct category.

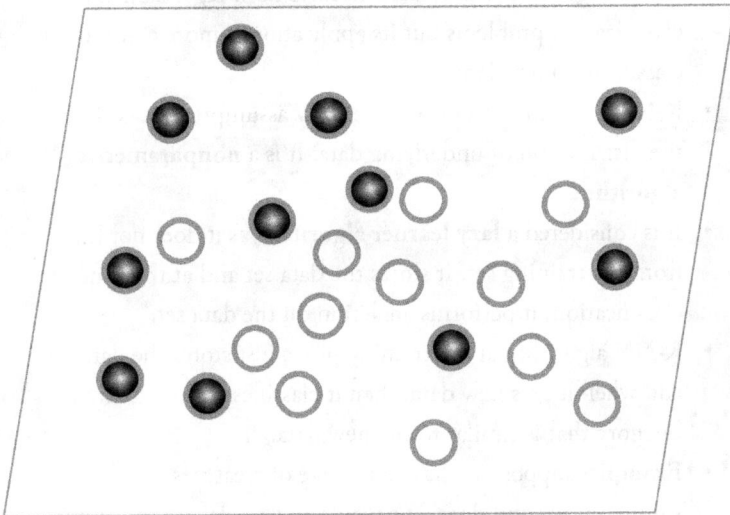

Figure 6.17 Two categories of data to classify

- Select a value of K where K is the number of the nearest neighbors to the data points in both classes and categories. The nearest neighbors are calculated using distance measures.
- Divide the data into training and test sets.
- **Step 2:** determine which distance function is to be used.

The following are the distance functions out of which the Euclidean distance is most used.

$$\textit{Euclidean Distance: } Dist(A,B) = \sqrt{\frac{\sum_{i=1}^{m}(x_i - y_i)^2}{m}} \qquad (6.23)$$

Manhattan Dist.

$$Dist. = \sum_{i=1}^{0} |X[i] - y[i]|$$

$$\textit{Correlation Dist.} = Dist - correlation\ (A,\ B) = \frac{\sum_{i=1}^{m}(x_i - \mu_i)(y_i - \mu_i)}{\sqrt{\sum_{i=1}^{m}(x_i - \mu_i)^2} * \sqrt{\sum_{i=1}^{m}(y_i - \mu_i)^2}}$$

$$\textit{Minkowsky distance: dist.} - Minkowsky\ (A,\ B) = \left(\sum_{i=1}^{m}|x_i - y_i|^r + b\right)^{1/r}$$

$$(6.24)$$

- Calculate the distance of **K number of neighbors,** that is, calculate the distance between the new data entry and all other existing data entries and arrange them in ascending order.
- The distance can be calculated using several measures. We have used the Euclidean distance.
- **Step 3:** determine the K-nearest neighbors as per the calculated distance.
- **Step 4:** among these K neighbors, count the number of data points in each category.

- **Step 5:** assign the new data point to that category for which the number of neighbor is maximum or assign the new data point or case to the majority class in the nearest neighbor or assign the test data/class based on a majority vote of its K neighbors. Figure 6.18 (A)–(C) explains the steps of the process.

Note: k-NN works well for a small number of data sets or input variables. k-NN makes no assumptions about the distribution or the data sets as it is a nonparametric method.

Factors Influencing the Outcomes:

1. The distance function or distance matrix is used to determine the nearest neighbors.
2. The number of neighbors (k) used to classify the new data point.

Choosing the Right Value for K

1. To determine the right value of K, the K-NN algorithm should be run several times with different values of K and select the K value that reduces the errors while maintaining the bias-variance trade-off.
2. Taking the value of K = 1 makes the prediction less stable. Increasing the value of K, the predictions become more stable and accurate due to majority voting. Higher values of K beyond a certain point may increase the number of errors.
3. The value of K should be an odd number to avoid ties.
4. A conventional way of finding k value is by using the expression: $K = \sqrt{n} / 2$ where n is the number of data points.
5. The data should be divided into training and validation sets. Usually, the test set is not used. The validation set is used to tune the value of K. Then select K that works for the data in question.
6. Note that K and K-NN algorithms are different and should not be confused with each other. For k means algorithm, a different method (Elbow) method is used to find k.

(A)

(B)

(C)

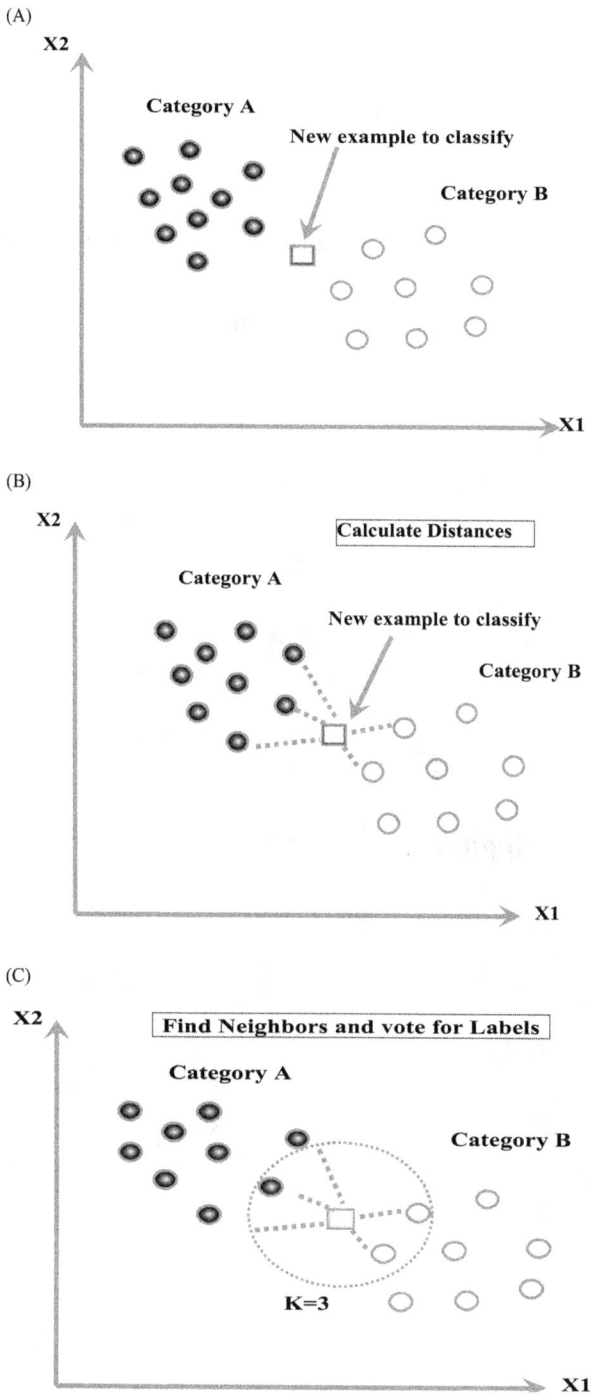

Figure 6.18 (A)–(C) The process explained

Another Example

1. Consider a data set with two classes or categories as shown below. A new data point or class has been introduced to the data set. This is represented by a square in Figure 6.19.
2. Assign a value to K where K is the number of neighbors to consider before classifying the new data entry. Here we assume the value of K is 3 as shown in Figure 6.20.
3. Since the value of K is 3, the algorithm will only consider the three nearest neighbors to the square point (new entry). This is represented in the graph above.
4. Out of the three nearest neighbors in Figure 6.20, the majority class is the class with dark circles so the new entry will be assigned to that class.
5. Therefore, the new data entry has been classified in category A with dark circles.

A numerical example: we present a numerical example here that demonstrates the calculations involved in this algorithm. Table 6.13

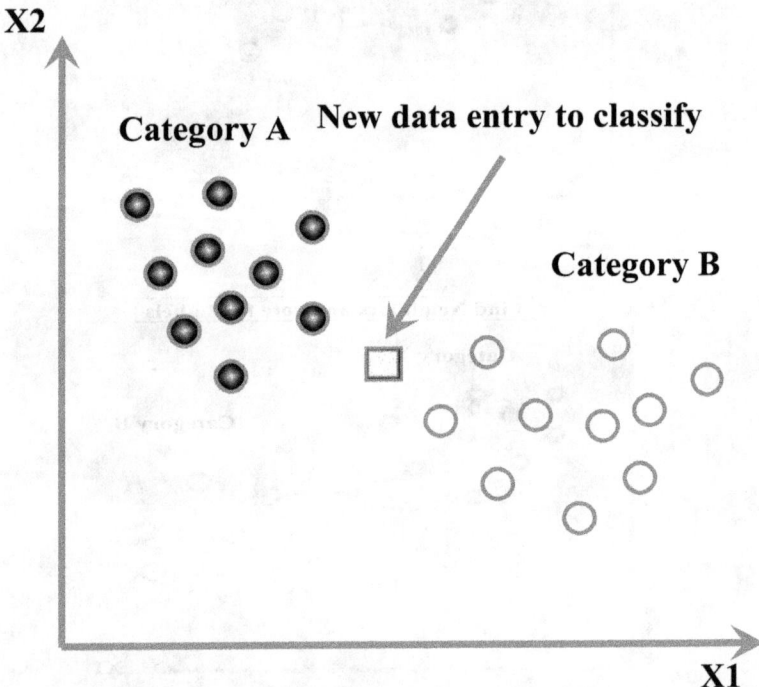

Figure 6.19 Categories A and B with new data point

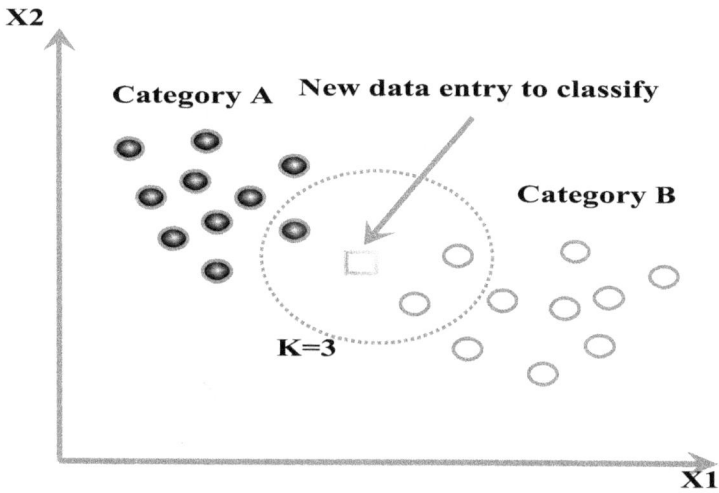

Figure 6.20 Selecting a value for K

represents a data set. The first two columns of the table show two features—**Height** (in centimeters) and **Weight** (in kilograms) of a certain
group of individuals. Each row in the table has a class of either **under-
weight (U) or normal weight (N)**. The problem is to classify a new

Table 6.13 Data for numerical example

(1) Height (cm)	(2) Weight (kg)	(3) Under Wt (U)/ Normal Wt (N)	(4) Distances	(5) Sorted Distances	(6) Rank	(7) Under Wt (U)/Normal Wt (N)
170	52	U	3.16	2.24	1.	U
185	63	N	17.89	3.16	2	N
178	69	N	16.64	4.12	3	N
175	65	N	11.66	4.47	4	N
176	57	U	7.28	7.28	5	U
179	55	U	10.00	8.54	6	U
170	59	N	4.12	10.00	7	N
177	58	N	8.54	11.66	8	N
173	53	U	4.47	16.64	9	U
171	54	U	2.24	17.89	10	U
169	55	?				

individual whose height and weight are given to one of the classes U or N. The new entry in **the last row of Table 6.13 shows the features of the new individual.** It shows that the person has a height of (169 cm) and a weight of (55 kg). We need to classify the individual to one of the U or N class.

- First, assume a value of K. Suppose this value is 4 or (**K** is 4).
- Next, to classify we need to calculate the distance from the new entry to other entries in the data set using the Euclidean distance formula. Figure 6.21 shows the distances to be calculated.
- Using the Euclidean distance formula, we calculate the distance of the new entry (169,55) to all the other points. Colum (4) of Table 6.13 shows the distances.
- Next, sort the distances in ascending or increasing order. The sorted distances are shown in Column (5) of Table 6.13.
- Rank these distances from the lowest to highest (see Column (6) of Table 6.13). Colum (7) of Table 6.13 shows the classification (U) or (N) from Colum (3) of Table 6.13.

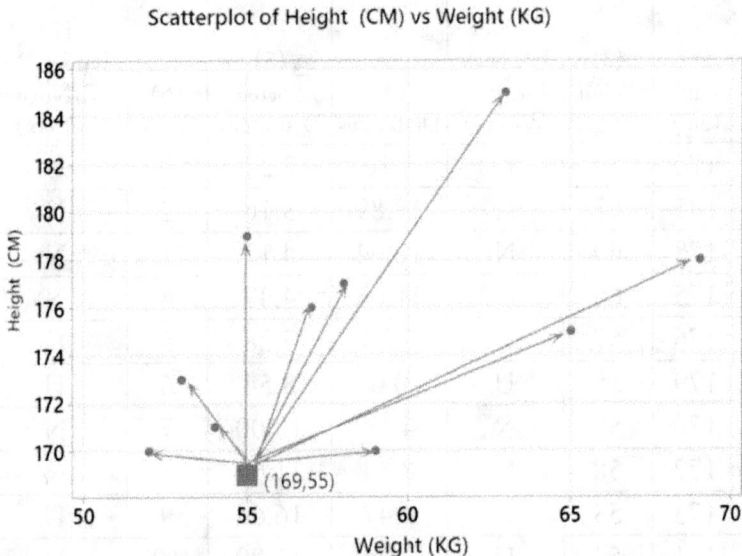

Figure 6.21 Distance of the new point to given points

- Since we chose 4 as the value of **K**, we will only consider the first four rows.
- We can see in Table 6.13, Column (7), that the majority class within the four nearest neighbors to the new entry is **N**. Therefore, we will classify the new entry as **N or Normal.**

Summary

This chapter discussed the most widely used important supervised learning models and their applications. The types of models in machine learning—supervised learning, unsupervised learning, semisupervised learning, and reinforcement learning—were explained with their applications and the types of problems they can solve.

This chapter focused on supervised learning models and their applications. The two major types of supervised learning models—regression and classification—were discussed. Several regression models and their variations are applied in machine learning. Among the widely used models, we discussed the following regression models and their evaluation criteria:

- Linear models: univariate linear regression model, least squares method, interpretation of models, the standard error of estimate, coefficient of determination R^2
- Multivariate regression models—n explanatory variables
- Ridge regression, multicollinearity and autocorrelation, effects of multicollinearity
- Nonlinear regression (quadratic regression)
- Other types of regression algorithms lasso and ridge regressions—L1 and L 2 regularizations, metrics to quantify performance (MSE, R^2 value, etc.)

The classification models applied to machine learning were explained with their applications and examples. The following classification models were discussed:

- Logistic regression—binary response variable
- LDA

- SVMs—hyperplane and kernelling, CART, decision trees
- Multivariate classification models, Naïve Bayes classifier
- k-nearest neighbors (KNN)
- Random forest classifier

CHAPTER 7

Unsupervised Learning Models

Chapter Highlights

- Unsupervised Learning
- Supervised Learning Versus Unsupervised learning
- Why Unsupervised Learning?
- Some Drawbacks of Unsupervised Learning
- Parametric Unsupervised Learning
- Nonparametric Unsupervised Learning
- Unsupervised Learning Models
- Types of Unsupervised Learning Algorithms
- Classical Unsupervised ML Problem: Clustering (Explanation, Motivation, etc.)
  - Hierarchical Clustering: Complete Linkage, Single Linkage, Average Linkage, Centroid Linkage
- K-means Clustering
- Principal Component Analysis
- Association Rules
- Summary

Unsupervised Learning

Unsupervised learning is a machine learning technique in which there is no known target. Unlike supervised learning models, which work on a known target where the users supervise the model, unsupervised learning techniques or models work on no known target or label. The users do not need to supervise these models. In unsupervised learning, the model works on its own to detect unknown patterns and information in the data that were previously unknown. While the supervised learning models work on labeled data or known targets, the unsupervised learning models mainly deal with the unlabeled data.

Unsupervised learning models try to find any similarities, differences, patterns, and structure in data by itself with no human intervention.

As an example of unsupervised learning, consider a child in a family with a pet dog. The child is very familiar with the dog and knows what a dog looks like but does not know that there are lots of other dogs that are different. Now, when the child sees another dog, he will still be able to recognize a dog with its features (two ears, four legs, tail, appearance, etc.). This type of prediction is known as unsupervised learning where the child is not told or trained as to what a dog looks like. If the child was trained to recognize a dog, it would be an example of a supervised learning problem.

Supervised Learning Versus Unsupervised Learning

The differences between unsupervised versus supervised learning are explained in Table 7.1.

Table 7.1 Differences between unsupervised vs supervised learning

	Unsupervised Learning	Supervised Learning
	The model tries to find patterns in the data without a label or target. This type of learning is done without human supervision.	The input data are labeled with answer keys telling the model the desired output.
	No label is provided (the data are unlabeled). Unsupervised learning is used to cluster information in data sets.	The data are labeled (the desired output is provided).
	The model is given input data (x) but no output or target. In other words, the data are not labeled.	The model is provided with input variables or features (x) and the output variable (desired output) or the target (y). The data are labeled in this case.

	Unsupervised Learning	Supervised Learning
	The unsupervised learning methods are applied to clustering and association problems.	Applied to classification and regression problems. Classification problems classify the data into one or the other group or to which class an instance belongs to. Regression problems are used to predict the future outcome (in many cases, the predict continuous variables, such as demand, sales, temperature, and so on.
	The desired results may not be as accurate.	Provides better accuracy in the results.
Common algorithms	Common classification algorithms are: <ul><li>Clustering (a technique that groups unlabeled data based on their similarities or differences)</li><li>K-means</li><li>Gaussian mixture models</li><li>Principal component analysis (dimensionality reduction)</li><li>Association rules</li></ul>	Common classification algorithms are logistic regression, support vector machines, decision tree classification, k-nearest neighbors, and others outlined as follows: <ul><li>Regression models (different types)</li><li>Linear discriminant analysis</li><li>Support vector machines</li><li>Decision trees</li><li>Naïve Bayes</li><li>Random forest</li></ul>
	Challenges of unsupervised learning: Unsupervised learning is more difficult and involved than supervised learning as it does not have a corresponding output. The unsupervised learning algorithm may be less accurate as input data are not labeled, and algorithms do not know the exact known output.	Challenges of **supervised learning:** Requires a huge amount of data. Nowadays, machine learning algorithms are trained with millions of data. Collecting and labeling huge quantity of data is involved and is a tedious process.
Applications	**Data labeling:** using clustering, the data are clustered and subsequently labeled.	Supervised learning models have been used to assist doctors to diagnose or predict disease in patients before they manifest.

(Continued)

Table 7.1 (Continued)

	Unsupervised Learning	**Supervised Learning**
	Image compression: unsupervised learning algorithms are used to reduce the number of dimensions in a data set preserving most of the information in the data. **Anomaly detection:** unsupervised learning models are used for anomaly detection (a method to detect outliers and unusual data points). Some other applications include: • data exploration, • customer segmentation, • recommender systems, • target marketing campaigns, • data preparation and visualization, and so on.	Other examples are spam detection (detect spam detection, sentiment detection, and self-driving cars)

Why Unsupervised Learning?

Here are prime reasons for using unsupervised learning in machine learning:

- Unsupervised learning is used to detect all kinds of unknown patterns in the data.
- Unsupervised learning is performed on unlabeled data that are easier to obtain and may be readily available from a computer.
- There are cases where it is difficult to determine the number of classes, or in how many classes the data should be divided into.
- Unsupervised learning is very useful for raw data exploration needs.
- Unsupervised methods may be helpful in finding features useful for categorization.
- Unsupervised methods are useful in searching for unknown similarities and differences in data and creating corresponding groups.
- The unsupervised method being used does not require training data to be labeled.

Some Drawbacks of Unsupervised Learning

- Unsupervised Learning is more complex compared to supervised learning tasks as no targets or labels in the data are available.
- It is difficult to be confident about the results as no labels are available to compare.
- Often external evaluation may be needed to justify the results.

Unsupervised learning may be parametric or nonparametric.

Parametric Unsupervised Learning

Parametric unsupervised learning assumes that the population from which the data are extracted follows a certain probability distribution that has a fixed set of parameters. For example, if the normality assumption holds and is appropriate, then the distribution is defined by a normal curve with parameters mean (μ) and standard deviation (σ). This implies that if the underlying distribution can be safely assumed to be normal, then the probability of any future observation can be determined using the mean and standard deviation of the data.

Parametric unsupervised learning enables the construction of Gaussian mixture models in which using expectation maximization algorithm can be used to predict the class of the sample in question. The parametric unsupervised model is involved and complex as there is no correct measure of accuracy in the absence of labels.

Nonparametric Unsupervised Learning

In this version of unsupervised learning, the data are grouped into clusters, where each cluster provides some information about categories and classes present in the data. The method is commonly used to model data with small sample sizes. As the name suggests, there is no underlying assumption regarding the distribution of the population from which the data come. Since there is no assumption about the distribution, the method is also referred to as a distribution-free method.

Unsupervised Learning Models

Types of Unsupervised Learning Algorithms

Clustering is the most widely used unsupervised learning problem. Unsupervised learning problems are generally grouped into clustering and association problems.

Clustering

A machine learning technique that groups *unlabeled* data based on their similarities or differences. Unsupervised learning is commonly used to cluster information in data sets. This method groups similar data points or objects into clusters that are not defined beforehand. In a cluster, the objects in the same group are more similar to each other than the objects in the other groups. The group of similar objects is called a **Cluster.**

In clustering, the technique or the model being used finds any patterns, similarities, and/or differences within uncategorized data. If any natural groups or classes exist in the data, the model detects them. Cluster analysis seeks to find clusters in the data without having to prespecify a set of categories.

Types of Clustering Algorithm

The following are the commonly used clustering algorithms used in Machine Learning:

- Hierarchical clustering
- K-means clustering
- Singular value decomposition
- Independent component analysis

We will discuss some of these algorithms here.

A well-known clustering algorithm is K-means. K-means clustering is a common example of an exclusive clustering method where data points are assigned into K groups, where K is the number of clusters based on the distance from each group's centroid. The data points closest to a given centroid will be clustered under the same category.

Hierarchical Clustering

The hierarchical clustering algorithm puts similar objects into groups called clusters. The outcome is a set of clusters where each cluster is distinct from each other cluster and the objects within each cluster are like each other. This method creates a hierarchy of clusters where two close clusters are in the same cluster. The algorithm ends when there is only one cluster left. The hierarchical clustering can be broadly divided into the following two groups:

(1) Agglomerative: it is a bottom-up approach, in which the algorithm starts with each data point as a single cluster and merges them until one cluster is left.

(2) Divisive: this algorithm is the reverse of the agglomerative algorithm. It is a top-down approach.

The **agglomerative hierarchical clustering** is the most common type of hierarchical clustering for grouping objects into clusters based on their similarity. It is also known as agglomerative nesting (AGNES). It is a bottom-up approach where each observation is its own cluster, and the pairs of clusters are merged as they move up in the hierarchy. The steps for this process are as follows:

1. Take each data point as a single-point cluster thus forming N number of clusters.

2. Take the two closest data points and make them one cluster forming N-1 clusters.

3. Take the two closest clusters and make them one cluster forming Forms N-2 clusters.

4. Repeat Step 3 until one cluster left.

Measuring the Distance Between Clusters

Different methods are used to decide the rules for forming clusters. These methods are known as linkage methods. The common linkage methods are as follows:

- **Complete linkage**: in this method, the distance between two clusters is defined as the *largest* distance between two points in each cluster.
- **Single linkage**: in this method, the distance between two clusters is the *shortest* distance between two points in each cluster.
- **Average linkage**: here, the distance between two clusters is defined as the average distance between each point in one cluster to every point in the other cluster.
- **Centroid-linkage**: this method finds the centroid of each cluster, for example, cluster 1 and cluster 2 and calculates the distance between the two before merging.

The use of these methods is the choice of the analyst. There are no guiding rules in guiding these methods, but different linkage methods may lead to different clusters.

These methods demonstrate how hierarchical clustering works. The entire process of this clustering method is usually demonstrated using a **dendrogram**, which is a tree diagram depicting the hierarchical relationships between sets of data. A dendrogram memorizes or stores the steps of the hierarchical clustering algorithm. A dendrogram is a pictorial description that shows how the cluster is formed.

K-means Clustering

K-means is a simple unsupervised learning algorithm. It classifies a given data set into K clusters where k is the number of clusters which is predetermined. The algorithm puts the data points into predefined clusters, K which is the input to this algorithm. Next, each data point is assigned to the nearest cluster center, called *centroids*. Figure 7.1 shows the clusters

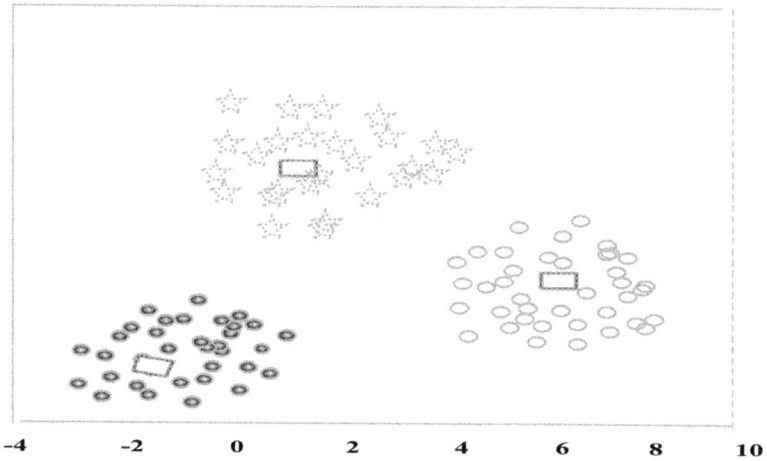

Figure 7.1 Clusters with centroids

with the black points as centroids. These centroids should be placed as far apart as possible. The choice of the centroids is critical as different locations of the centroids produce different results. The placement of the centroids far away from each other produces a better and consistent result. The data points are assigned to one of the k groups. In k-means clustering, each group is defined by creating a centroid for each group. The closest points to the centroid are added to form the clusters.

k-means clustering aims to group n observations into k clusters in which each observation belongs to the cluster with the nearest mean (cluster centers or *centroid*). The process of grouping the points in the clusters is done in a way that objects in the same cluster are more similar to each other compared to other clusters.

The *k*-means clustering minimizes within-cluster variances (squared Euclidean distances). This model is similar to the Gaussian mixture model. Both of these models use the centroid or the cluster centers to model the data. While k-means clustering tends to find clusters of comparable spatial extent, the Gaussian mixture model can model the clusters with different shapes.

The *k*-means algorithm is somewhat related to the *k-nearest neighbor classifier*, which is a popular supervised machine learning technique for classification that is often confused with *k*-means due to its name.

In K-means, we take each point belonging to a given data set and associate it to the nearest centroid. When all points are assigned, the first step is completed, and the initial grouping is done. Next, we recalculate k new centroids as centers of the clusters resulting from the previous step. Once we have the new centroids, a new grouping is to be made between the same data points and the nearest new centroid. This creates a loop. The k centroids may change their location until no more changes can be made, that is, centroids do not move anymore.

K-means is an algorithm for exclusive clustering, also known as partitioning or segmentation.

Steps of the K-Means Clustering Algorithm

Step 1: select K – the number of clusters the data will be divided into.

Step 2: select k random points or determine the centroids for each cluster.

Step 3: assign each data point to its closest centroid from the predefined K clusters.

Step 4: calculate the variance and place a new centroid of each cluster.

Step 5: repeat Step 3, that is, reassigning each datapoint to the new closest centroid of each cluster.

Step 6: if any reassignment occurs, then go to Step 4 or else FINISH.

Step 7: finish.

K-means steps are shown visually in Figures 7.2 and 7.3.

Suppose we have two variables X1 and X2. The x–y axis scatter plot of these two is shown in Figure 7.4. We need to choose some K random points or centroids from the clusters. These points can be either the points from the data set or any other point. Refer to Figure 7.5.

- Suppose we select k number of clusters, that is, K = 2, to identify the data set and put them into different clusters. This means we will try to group these data sets into two different clusters.
- We need to choose some K random points or centroid to form the cluster. These points can be either the points from

Before K-Means

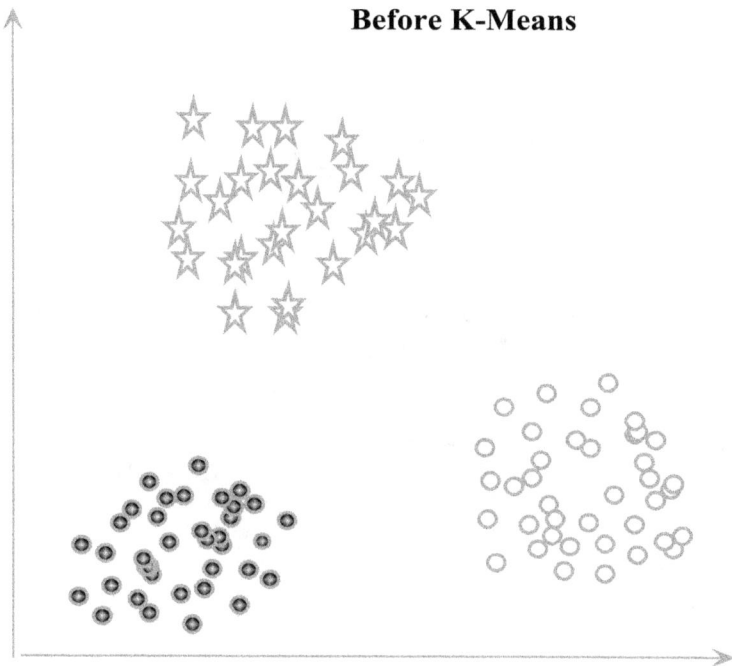

Figure 7.2 Before applying K-means

After K-Means

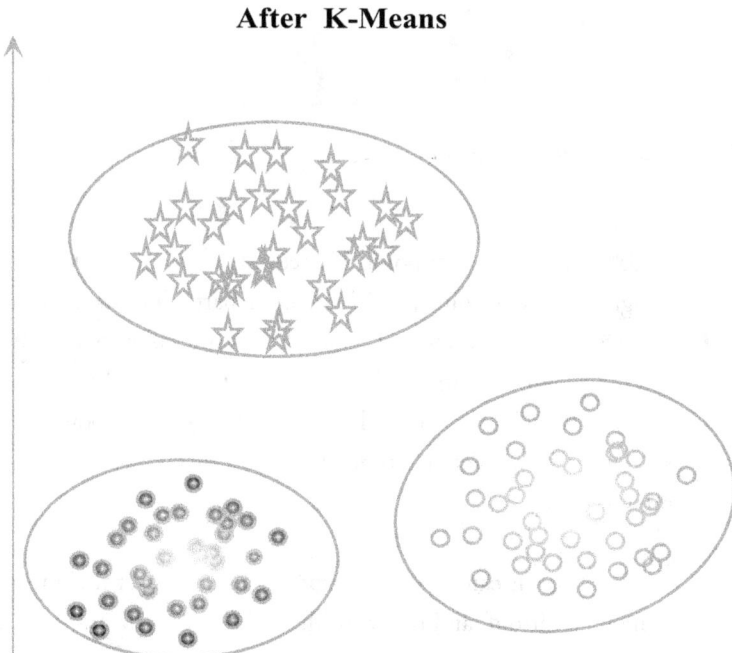

Figure 7.3 After applying K-means

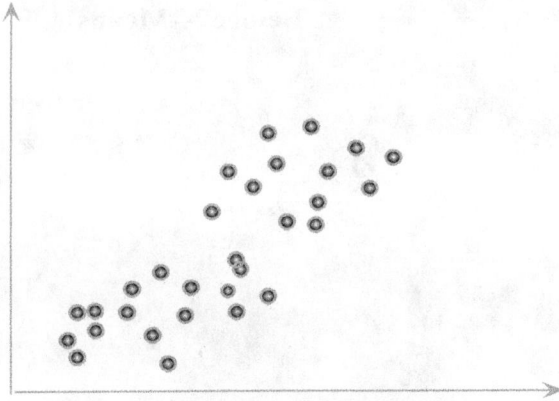

Figure 7.4 Scatter plot of variable

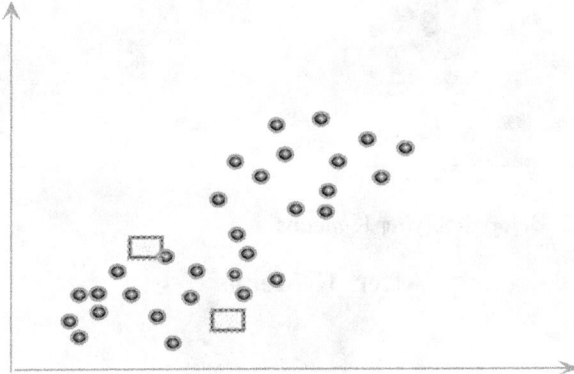

Figure 7.5 Selected two points

the data set or any other point. We select two points (shown in Figure 7.5) as k points, which are not a part of our data set.

- Now we will assign each data point of the scatter plot to its closest K-point or centroid. We will calculate it using the distance formula to calculate the distance between two points. Next, we draw a median between both the centroids as shown in Figure 7.6.

From Figure 7.6, it can be seen that points to the left of the line are closer to the K1 centroid, and points to the right of the line are close to the K2 centroid.

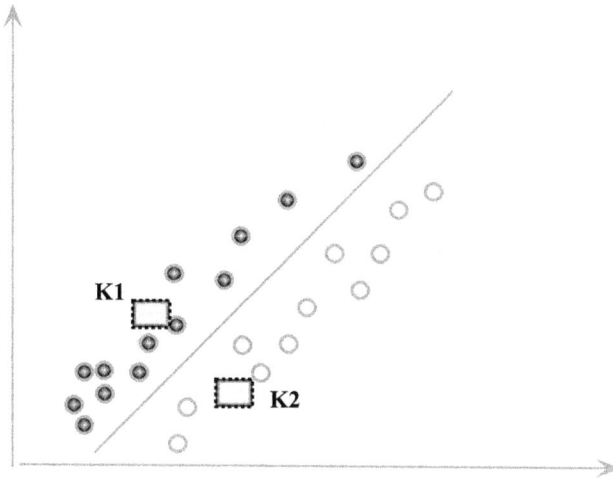

Figure 7.6 Centroid with median line

Since we need to find the closest cluster, we will repeat the process by choosing **a new centroid**. To choose the new centroids, we will compute the center of gravity of these centroids to find new centroids shown in Figure 7.7.

- The next step is to reassign each data point to the new centroid. For this, we repeat the same process of finding a median line earlier. The median will be as shown in Figure 7.8.
- From Figure 7.8, we can see that one point (denoted by a blank circle) is on the left side of the line and two points denoted by black circles are right to the line. These three points will be assigned to new centroids.
- As reassignment takes place, we again go to Step 4, of finding new centroids or K-points.

The process is repeated by finding the center of gravity of centroids. The new centroids will be as shown in Figure 7.9.

- We get the new centroids, draw the median line, and reassign the data points. See Figure 7.10.

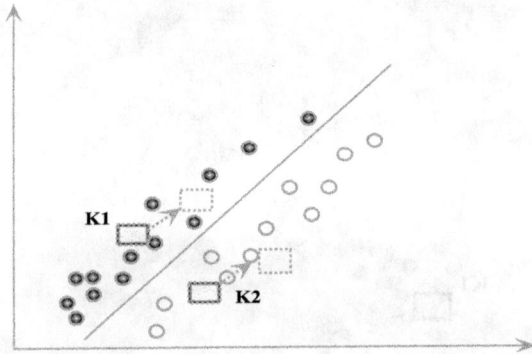

Figure 7.7 New centroid with median line

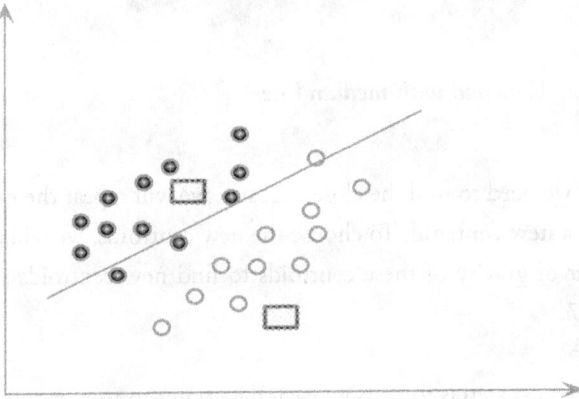

Figure 7.8 Data points assigned and new median line

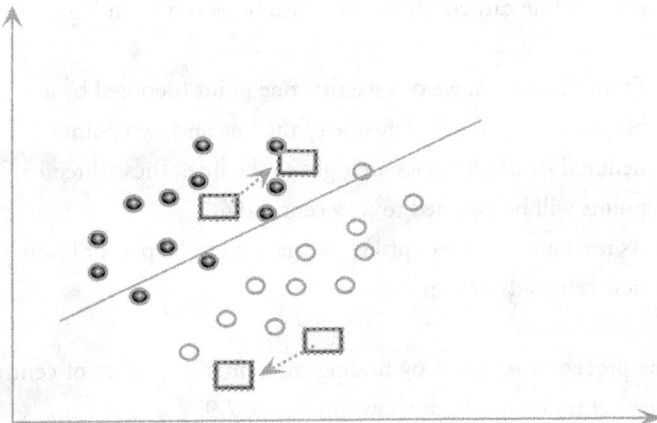

Figure 7.9 The new centroids

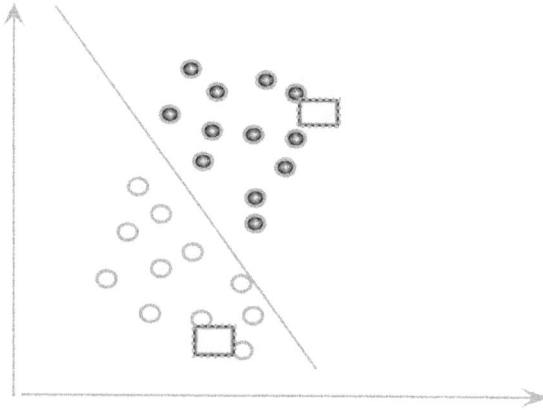

Figure 7.10 New centroid and median line

From Figure 7.10 we can see that there are no dissimilar data points on either side of the line. This means the model is complete and clusters are created. See Figure 7.11.

Figure 7.12 shows the final clusters with the centroids removed.

How to Choose the Value of *K Number of Clusters* in K-means Clustering?

The performance of the K-means clustering algorithm depends on forming highly efficient clusters. Selecting the optimal number of clusters is a big task. There are different ways of finding the optimal number of clusters, K. One widely used method is known as the elbow method described below.

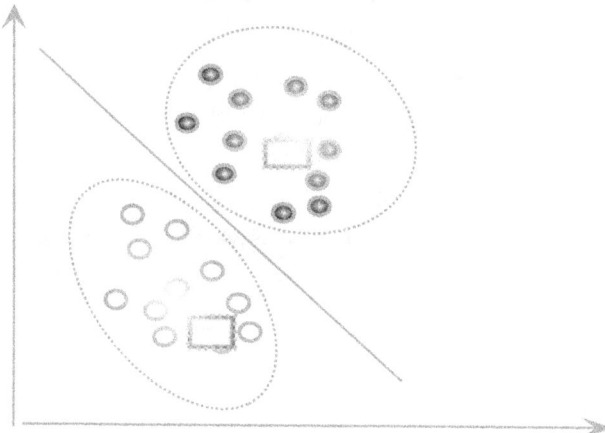

Figure 7.11 The created clusters

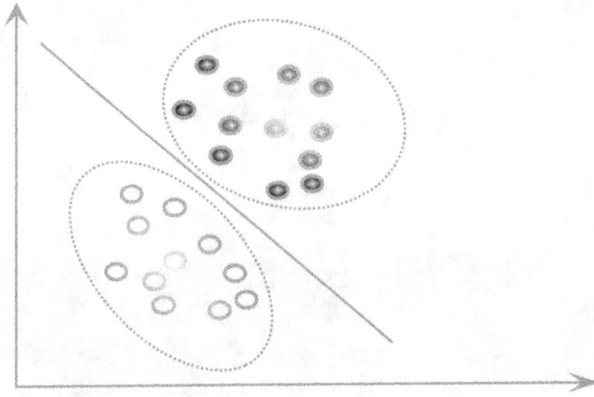

Figure 7.12 The final clusters

Elbow Method

The elbow method is one of the most popular ways to find the optimal number of clusters. This method uses the concept of WCSS value. **WCSS** stands for **Within Cluster Sum of Squares**, which defines the total variations within a cluster. The formula to calculate the value of WCSS (for three clusters) is given below:

$$\text{WCSS} = \sum_{\text{Pi in Cluster1}} \text{distance } (P_i\ C_1)^2 + \sum_{\text{Pi in Cluster2}} \text{distance } (P_i\ C_2)^2 + \sum_{\text{Pi in CLuster3}} \text{distance } (P_i\ C_3)^2$$

In the above formula of WCSS,

$\sum_{\text{Pi in Cluster1}} \text{distance } (P_i\ C_1)^2$ is the sum of the square of the distances between each data point and its centroid within Cluster1, and the same is for the other two terms.

To measure the distance between data points and centroid, we can use any method such as Euclidean distance or Manhattan distance.

To find the optimal value of clusters, the elbow method follows the steps as given:

- It executes the K-means clustering on a given data set for different K values (ranges from 1 to 10).
- For each value of K, we calculate the WCSS value.

- Next, we plot a curve between calculated WCSS values and the number of clusters K.
- The sharp point of bend or a point of the plot looks like an arm, then that point is considered as the best value of K.

Since the graph shows the sharp bend, which looks like an elbow, it is known as the elbow method. The graph for the elbow method looks similar to Figure 7.13.

Principal Component Analysis (PCA)

PCA is a dimensionality reduction method that is often used to reduce the dimensionality of large data sets by transforming a large set of variables into a smaller set while maintaining most of the information in the data. PCA helps to identify the most common dimensions of the data, thereby making the analysis easier.

PCA is used to identify a smaller number of uncorrelated variables, called *principal components*, from a large set of data. With this analysis, we can create new variables or principal components that are linear combinations of the observed variables. The objective of PCA is to explain the maximum amount of variance with the least number of principal components.

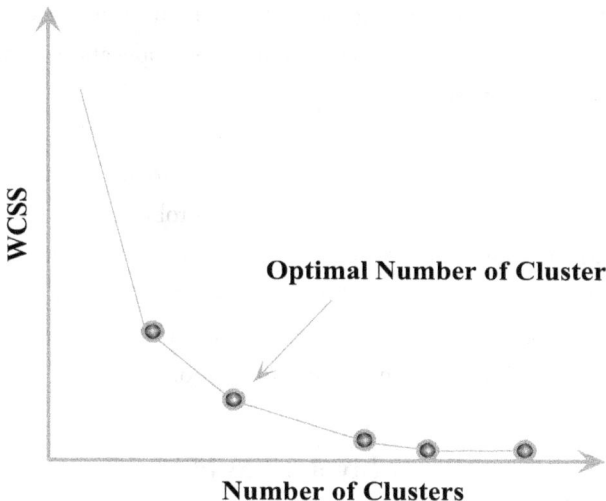

Figure 7.13 *Determining optimal number of clusters, K*

For example, we can use the PCA to analyze customer responses to several characteristics of a new product. In this case, we would like to form a smaller number of uncorrelated variables that are easier to interpret and analyze than the large number of observed variables the data are collected on.

PCA is commonly used as one of the steps in a series of analyses. For example, principal components can be used before regression analysis to determine and avoid multicollinearity. This is also done to reduce the number of predictors.

In machine learning projects, it is not uncommon to have data with a very large number of variables or features. It is often the case that all the variables are not critical and all the variables in the model may not contribute to the model. Including all the features may increase the model's complexity and interpretation. The method of principal component analysis can be used to detect and eliminate less important variables and retain the critical variables.

PCA is also known *as dimensionality reduction* method as it eliminates the less important variables from the model. Reducing the number of variables or features or eliminating the noncritical or less important variables that may not contribute to the model makes exploration and visualization more transparent. It also makes the analysis and interpretation easier. PCA analyzes all the features in the data and eliminates unnecessary features while preserving the exact information in the data. Here we discuss the PCA applications briefly and their applications in machine learning. Here are a few of PCA applications:

- PCA has applications in face recognition problem, image identification, pattern recognition, and problems where a huge amount of data with numerous features are needed.
- This machine learning technique makes the data more manageable by reducing the number of variables of a large data set with minimum loss of information.

Steps Involved in PCA

Figure 7.14 shows the steps of PCA.

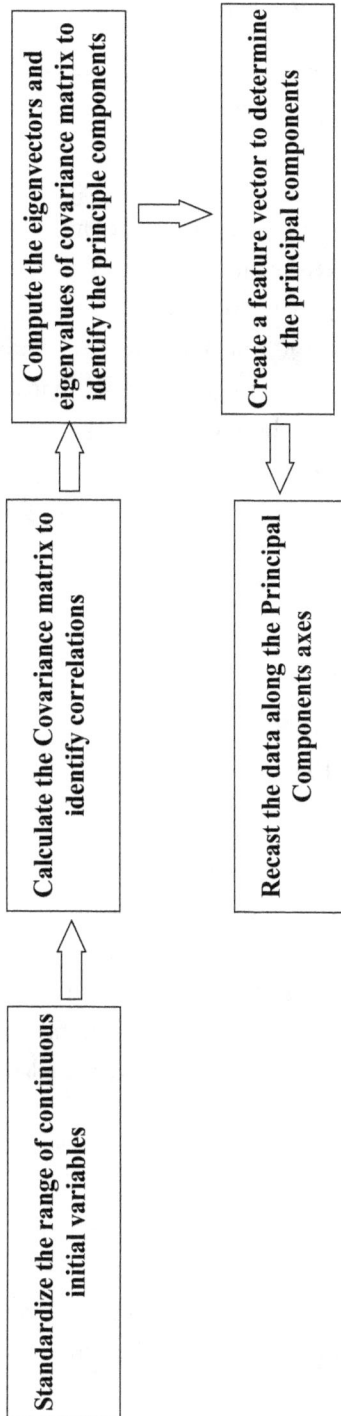

Figure 7.14 The principal component analysis (PCA) process

Step 1: Standardizing the Variables

In this process, the range of variables is calculated and standardized. By standardizing the range of continuous variables, each data point contributes equally to the analysis.

The reason for performing standardization is that the standardized data are quite sensitive to the variances of the initial variables. If there are large differences between the ranges of initial variables, the variables with larger ranges will dominate over those with small ranges (a variable that ranges between 0 and 100 will dominate over a variable that ranges between 0 and 1). This will lead to biased results. Transforming the data to a scale of 0 to 1 overcomes this problem.

The data can be standardized using a simple formula shown below. It is done by subtracting each value from the mean of the variable and dividing the result by the standard deviation of the variable or,

$$z = \frac{x_i - \text{mean}}{\text{Standard deviation}}$$

Standardization transforms all the variables to the same scale.

Step 2: Calculating the Covariance Matrix

The covariance matrix summarizes the correlations between all possible pairs of variables. The aim of the covariance matrix is to understand how the variables of the input data vary from the mean with respect to each other or to see if there is any relationship between them. In cases where variables are highly correlated, they contain redundant information. To understand the relationship between the variables, the correlation matrix is calculated. The sign of the covariance defines the relationship between the variables.

- If the sign of the covariance between the two variables is positive, then the two variables increase or decrease together (positively correlated).
- If the sign is negative, it is an indication that as one variable increases, the other decreases (inversely correlated).

In summary, the covariance matrix helps to identify how the variables of the given data vary from the mean value of the variable, sort out any inter-related variables, and segregate the highly inter-related variables.

The covariance matrix is a $p \times p$ symmetric matrix (where p is the number of dimensions). It has the covariances associated with all possible pairs of the initial variables. For example, for a three-dimensional data set with three variables x, y, and z, the covariance matrix is a 3×3 data matrix:

$$\begin{bmatrix} \text{cov}(x,x) & \text{cov}(x,y) & \text{cov}(x,z) \\ \text{cov}(y,x) & \text{cov}(y,y) & \text{cov}(y,z) \\ \text{cov}(z,x) & \text{cov}(z,y) & \text{cov}(z,z) \end{bmatrix}$$

For n observations $(x_1, y_1), (x_2, y_2), (x_n, y_n)$, the *covariance* is defined using the following relationship:

$$\text{cov}(x,y) = \frac{\sum (x_i - \bar{x})(y_i - \bar{y})}{n-1} \quad \text{or,} \quad \text{cov}(x,y) = \frac{\sum (x_i - \bar{x})(y_i - \bar{y})}{N}$$

- Note: the covariance of a number with itself is its variance, or $\text{cov}(x, x) = \text{var}(x)$.
- Similarly, the values of the covariance matrix at the main diagonal will be symmetric as the covariance is commutative $\text{cov}(x, y) = \text{cov}(y, x)$.
- If the value of the covariance in the matrix is positive, the variables are positively correlated. (That is, as x increases, y also increases and vice versa.)
- If the value of the covariance in the covariance matrix is negative, the variables are inversely correlated. (That is, as x increases, y decreases and vice versa.)
- The entries of the covariance matrix are symmetric with respect to the main diagonal, which means that the upper and the lower triangular portions are equal.

The calculated covariance matrix contains useful information regarding the relationship between the pairs of variables. It tells which pair of variables are correlated. This may be helpful in categorizing the variables.

The covariance matrix for four features, F1 to F4, will have the following form:

	F1	F2	F3	F4
F1	Var (F1)	Cov (F1, F2)	Cov (F1, F3)	Cov (F1, F4)
F2	Cov (F2, F1)	Var F2)	Cov (F2, F3)	Cov (F2, F4)
F3	Cov (F3, F1)	Cov (F3, F2)	Var (F3)	Cov (F3, F4)
F4	Cov (F4, F1)	Cov (F4, F2)	Cov (F4, F3)	Var (F4)

Once the covariance matrix is calculated, we have the correlations between all the possible pairs of variables summarized. We move to the next step.

Step 3: Compute the Eigenvectors and Eigenvalues of the Covariance Matrix to Identify the Principal Components

In this step, we need to calculate the eigenvectors and eigenvalues from the covariance matrix to determine the ***principal components*** of the data. Principal components are new variables that are constructed as linear combinations of the initial variables. These combinations are constructed such that the new variables or the principal components are uncorrelated and most of the information is contained in the first components. For example, 10-dimensional data will have 10 principal components, but the PCA puts the maximum possible information in the first component, then the maximum remaining information in the second, and so on.

- It determine the principal components of variables, we define eigenvalue and eigenvectors from the covariance matrix. Let M be any square matrix. A nonzero vector v is an eigenvector of A if,

$$Mv = \lambda v$$

for some value λ, called the corresponding eigenvalue.

5. Once the eigenvector components are calculated, we define eigenvalues in descending order (for all variables) that will give a list of principal components.

6. The eigenvalues represent the principal components and these components represent the direction of data.

7. If the line contains large variables of large variances, then there are many data points on the line. This means that there is more information on the line too.

8. Finally, these principal components form a line of new axes for easier evaluation of data. Also, the differences between the observations can be easily monitored.

PCA works by considering the variance of each feature as the high attribute variance shows a good split between the classes, and hence it reduces the dimensionality. Some real-world applications of PCA are image processing, movie recommendation systems, and optimizing the power allocation in various communication channels.

Anomaly Detection

Unsupervised learning models are used for anomaly detection (a method to detect outliers and unusual data points). Some other applications include:

- data exploration,
- customer segmentation,
- recommender systems,
- target marketing campaigns,
- data preparation and visualization, and so on.

Summary

The focus of this chapter was unsupervised learning and the types of unsupervised learning models. Unsupervised learning models try to find any similarities, differences, patterns, and structures in data by itself with no human intervention. The chapter outlined the differences between supervised and unsupervised learning and the needs and importance of unsupervised learning. We also discussed some drawbacks of this type of learning and the different types including the parametric and nonparametric unsupervised learning. Finally, the chapter explained the widely used unsupervised learning algorithms used to solve machine learning problems. The classical unsupervised learning models discussed in this chapter are clustering, hierarchical clustering: complete linkage, single linkage, average linkage, and centroid linkage. The other widely used models include K-means clustering, PCA and association rule.

CHAPTER 8

Supervised Learning Models Deep Learning Models

Chapter Highlights

- Neural Network Fundamentals
  - Neurons
  - Perceptrons
  - Activation Functions
- Neural Network Architectures
  - Multilayer Perceptrons (MLP)
  - Convolutional Neural Networks (CNN)
  - Other Common Neural Network Architectures

Neural Network Fundamentals

Humans possess the ability to process vast amounts of information (e.g., through our senses) and make complex decisions in a matter of seconds. Our brains consist of billions of interconnected neurons that work together to create a complex network responsible for our cognition, perception, and behavior. Inspired by the workings of biological neural networks, artificial neural networks (ANNs) have been developed to mimic the behavior of biological neurons in the brain. Despite the recent surge of interest in ANNs, their initial development dates as far back as the 1940s. Since then, ANNs have experienced tremendous acceleration in development and application.

ANNs form the basis of deep learning, which refers to the development of very large ANN models (we will revisit this definition as we develop more principles behind ANNs). Today, deep learning models are used in a wide range of applications. For example, deep learning models are used for image classification in self-driving cars, recommendation systems on streaming services, and natural language processing in large language models. They are one of the most versatile models that we have looked at thus far because they are capable of functioning in a variety of ways. Moreover, ANNs can be used for supervised learning (including both classification and regression), unsupervised learning, semi supervised learning, or a combination of these types simultaneously.

ANNs are composed of several components that together constitute the entire network. We will first introduce each component individually and later discuss how they all fit together to make different types of neural networks.

Neurons: artificial neurons are modeled after biological neurons in the human brain, and they function as the building blocks of ANNs. Specifically, each neuron takes in some input, which is typically the output from a previous neuron, applies one or more mathematical operations to it, and produces an output. An activation function is applied to the output of the neuron to determine whether the neuron will *fire* or not similar to the behavior of biological neurons.

Perceptrons: they are the simplest form of a neuron and are commonly found in all ANN models. Each perceptron has its own set of weights, where w_i represents the *ith* weight, and bias, $x_1, x_2, ... x_n$. An input sequence, , is inputted into the perceptron, which then outputs the dot product between the inputs and the weights summed with the bias after it passes through an activation function f(). Mathematically, the output of the perceptron is represented as $o = f(y) = f\left(\sum_{i=1}^{n} x_i w_i + b\right)$. Figure 8.1 shows the visual representation of a perceptron. The input sequence, $x_1, x_2, ... x_n$, is typically the output from the previous perceptron(s); the weights and bias values are local to each perceptron. These weight values are calculated during *training* of the neural network, which will be further discussed in Chapter 9.

Activation functions: these are mathematical functions applied to the outputs of perceptrons. Their purpose is to introduce nonlinear functionality into neural networks to make predictions that may not be possible by linear models. For example, if we consider the weighted sum operation of the perceptron $y = \sum_{i=1}^{n} x_i w_i + b$, without the activation function f(.), this model is identical to a linear

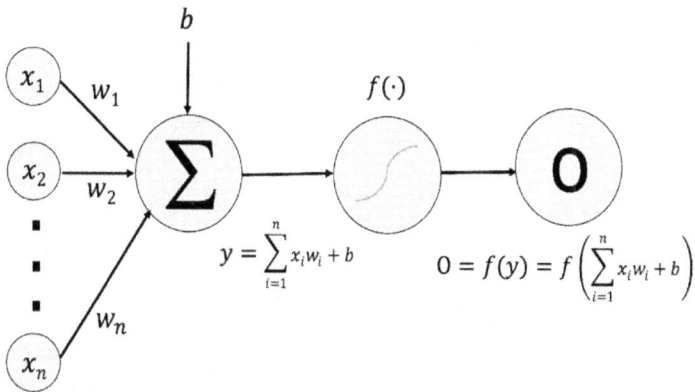

$$y = \sum_{i=1}^{n} x_i w_i + b$$

$$0 = f(y) = f\left(\sum_{i=1}^{n} x_i w_i + b\right)$$

Figure 8.1 The perceptron operation

regression model, where the w_i's represent the coefficients, x_i's are the inputs, and b is the intercept term. However, without any nonlinear functionality, this model alone can only find linear decision boundaries. In machine learning, we are often interested in classifying data that cannot be separated by straight lines and thus require some notion of nonlinear functionality (see Figure 8.2). Activation functions provide this nonlinear behavior and allow neural networks to learn complex nonlinear decision boundaries between data points by cascading several perceptrons, which are alternate performing linear and nonlinear operations.

Several types of activation functions are used in neural networks. Some common choices of activation functions are shown in Figure 8.3 and described below.

Sigmoid: the sigmoid activation function is given by $f(y) = \dfrac{1}{1+e^{-y}}$, where y is the input to the activation function and $e \approx 2.72$ is the exponential constant. The domain of the sigmoid function is all real numbers $(-\infty, +\infty)$ and the range is bounded between 0 and 1 $(0, +1)$. Specifically, for very small inputs (i.e., large negative values), the sigmoid is lower bounded by 0 whereas for very large inputs (i.e., large positive values), the sigmoid is upper bounded by 1. However, for input values between -5 and $+5$, the sigmoid acti-

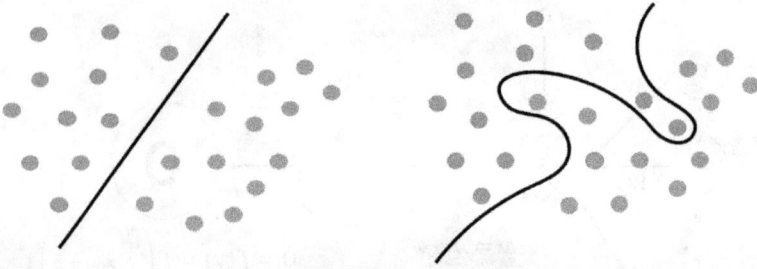

Figure 8.2 *Any machine learning classification algorithm without nonlinear functionality can only learn linear decision boundaries to discern data points (left). Real-world data may be separated through nonlinear decision boundaries (right). Such boundaries can only be learned through nonlinear activation functions utilized in neural networks*

vation provides close to a linear response as shown in Figure 8.3. Thus, the sigmoid activation function has a linear region (when the input is between –5 and +5) and a nonlinear region (when the input is less than –10 and greater than +10).

Hyperbolic tangent (tanh): the hyperbolic tangent, or tanh for short, function is given by $f(y) = \tanh(y) = \dfrac{e^y - e^{-y}}{e^y + e^{-y}}$. The domain of the tanh function is all real number $(-\infty, +\infty)$ and the range is bounded between –1 and +1 $(-1, +1)$. The behavior of the tanh function is similar to that of the sigmoid function in that it consists of a linear region close to the origin and a nonlinear region for large and small input values.

Rectified linear unit (ReLU): The ReLU activation function, similar to the tanh and sigmoid activation functions, consists of a linear and nonlinear region. The ReLU function is given by $f(y) = \max(0, y)$. That is, for any negative input, the ReLU outputs the value 0, and for all other values, the ReLU returns in the input value as the output. The ReLU is the most commonly used activation function in neural networks.

Leaky ReLU: The leaky ReLU is a modification of the ReLU activation function, and it is given by,

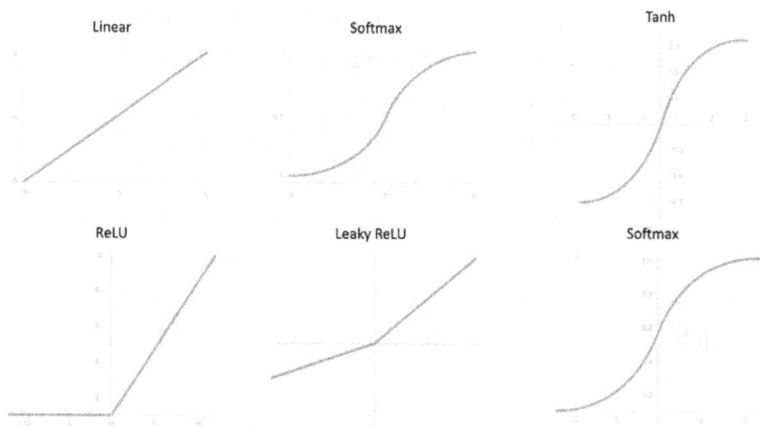

Figure 8.3 *Plots of commonly used activation functions in neural networks. Plots adapted from www.v7labs.com/blog/neural-networks-activation-functions*

$$f(y) = \begin{cases} \alpha y & y < 0 \\ y & y \geq 0 \end{cases},$$

α is a constant that is determined by the engineer. This activation function scales non negative values (by α) rather than outputting zero as the regular ReLU activation function does.

Softmax: the softmax function is a mathematical function commonly used in neural networks to convert a vector of numbers into a vector of probabilities. A vector of probabilities allows us to choose the element with the highest value as the *decision* made by a neural network, whereas it is much more difficult to compare numbers that may be very small, large, positive, or negative, as is the case when examining a vector of numbers. The softmax activation function is given by

$$f(y)_i = \frac{e^{y_i}}{\sum_{j=1}^{k} e^{y_j}},$$

Let us break down and understand each part of this equation. Notice that the input to this activation function is a bold y, which denotes a vector rather than a single number. It can have an arbitrary number of elements (e.g., $y = [y_1, y_2, \dots y_n]$, where each y_i is a single number). Now, the softmax function operates by exponentiating each element of the input vector in the numerator, which results in a set of positive numbers. It then normalizes these numbers by dividing each exponentiated value by the sum of all the exponentiated values in the denominator. This normalization ensures that all entries in the resulting output vector sum up to 1. As a result of this normalization, the output vector represents a valid probability space, where each element is between 0 and 1 and the total elements sum to 1.

Neural Network Architectures

Neural network architectures serve as blueprints that define the organization and flow of information in a neural network. Various types of neural network architectures exist such as multilayer perceptrons (MLPs), convolutional neural networks (CNNs), and recurrent neural networks (RNNs). Each architecture is best suited for different machine learning tasks, which will be further discussed in this chapter. Neural networks are composed of several layers, where each layer consists of different operation units such as perceptrons. Moreover, neural network architectures can differ in the type of operational unit that composes each layer. The number of layers in a neural network determines its depth. As more layers are added to a neural network architecture, the deeper it gets. This has coined the term *deep learning*, which refers to employing neural network architectures with several layers. In the remainder of this chapter, we will present an in-depth discussion on the two most common deep learning architectures (the MLP and the CNN) followed by a brief introduction to other commonly used neural network architectures.

Multilayer Perceptron (MLP)

The most common type of neural network architecture is the MLP, which is shown in Figure 8.4. MLPs consist of an input layer, one or more hidden layers, and an output layer. Each layer is composed of a set of perceptrons. The input layer serves as the entry point for data. As shown in

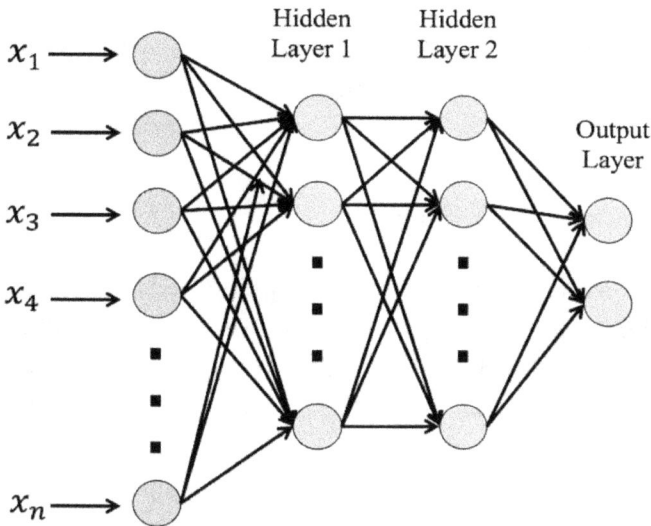

Figure 8.4 The architecture of an MLP with two hidden layers.
Each unit performs the operations of the perceptron shown in Figure
8.1

Figure 8.4, each perceptron in the input layer takes one feature as input and produces an output by multiplying it by a weight, adding a bias, and passing it through an activation function (i.e., the typical operations performed by a perceptron). The output of the perceptrons in the input layer is then passed to the hidden layers. Each perceptron in a given hidden layer receives all outputs from the perceptrons in the preceding layer as input produces a single output. Finally, the last hidden layer feeds its outputs to the output layer, which provides the final result or prediction based on the information processed by the preceding layers.

MLPs are characterized by their weights and biases. These parameters are adjusted using a set of labeled training data during the training process. The training process is an iterative approach, which gradually tunes the MLP's parameters (weights and biases) to output the correct label given an input. We will discuss the training process in greater depth in Chapter 9.

MLPs have found extensive applications across various domains including computer vision, natural language processing, finance, and many others. Their flexibility, scalability, and ability to handle high-dimensional data make them well-suited for tackling a range of real-world problems. Furthermore, advancements in computing power and the availability of vast amounts of data have contributed to the increased adoption and success of MLPs in recent years. Now, let us look at an example that an MLP could be deployed for.

Example 8.1: Let us consider the task of classifying handwritten digits into one of 10 categories (i.e., the digits 0 to 9) as a machine learning task that we would like to construct an MLP to perform. That is, given an image of a handwritten digit, we would like the MLP to predict which digit is between 0 and 9. Images of handwritten digits are shown in Figure 8.5. Each digit is similar but will vary slightly because every human's

Figure 8.5 *Sample images of hand-written digits from the MNIST data set*

Image Source: Baldominos (2019). A Survey of Handwritten Character Recognition with MNIST and EMNIST. https://en.wikipedia.org/wiki/MNIST_database

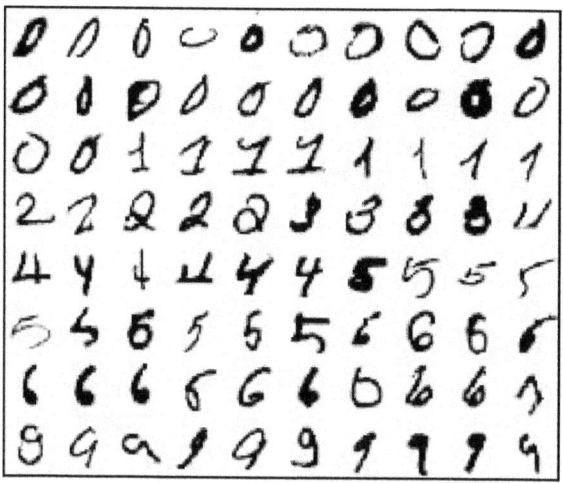

Figure 8.6 *Selected samples from the MNIST data set that are difficult to classify (for both humans and computers as well)*

Image Source: Krawiec (2001). Constructive Induction in Learning of Image Representation.

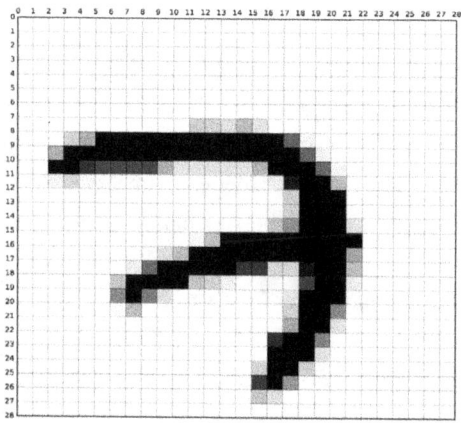

Figure 8.7 *An image from the MNIST data set shown in a grid, where each grid represents a pixel. Each grid value is a number between 0 and 255 representing the pixel intensity of the corresponding pixel*

Image Source: Baldominos, A. "A Survey of Handwritten Character Recognition With MNIST and EMNIST," *Applied Sciences*.

handwriting is slightly different. Thus, this is an ideal task for an MLP to perform to mimic human intelligence as humans are capable of easily distinguishing handwritten digits written by different people. However, for humans, this is only possible when the handwriting of the digit is legible. For example, the images shown in Figure 8.6 are digits that may be difficult for a human to read. We will see that an MLP may face the same problem.

We begin by considering each handwritten digit as a low-resolution 28 × 28 grayscale image. In computers, each image is stored as an array of numbers with each value denoting the pixel intensity, which varies between 0 and 255 in integer values. Thus, each image of these hand-written digits is seen by a computer as a 28 × 28 matrix (this process is visualized in Figure 8.7). However, since we are working with MLPs, it is difficult to input a matrix into the model. Instead, we will stack each column of the image matrix vertically to form a single vector with 28 × 28 = 784 *features*. Recalling a *feature* is just one of the inputs into a machine learning model. Typically, we have multiple features and can have hundreds or thousands of features as input. In this case, the features will be the pixel values of each image. This is typically how images are processed in computer vision applications.

Next, we need to quantitively label the images with their corresponding outputs. In this case, we can label each image as the number that is written in the image. Thus, the label of a handwritten "0" would be 0, the

Table 8.1 Conversion of integer labels to one-hot encoded labels

Integer Label	One-hot Encoded Label
0	1 0 0 0 0 0 0 0 0 0
1	0 1 0 0 0 0 0 0 0 0
2	0 0 1 0 0 0 0 0 0 0
3	0 0 0 1 0 0 0 0 0 0
4	0 0 0 0 1 0 0 0 0 0
5	0 0 0 0 0 1 0 0 0 0
6	0 0 0 0 0 0 1 0 0 0
7	0 0 0 0 0 0 0 1 0 0
8	0 0 0 0 0 0 0 0 1 0
9	0 0 0 0 0 0 0 0 0 1

label of a handwritten "1" would be a 1, and so on. However, we often use *one-hot encoding* to label the outputs for neural networks. One-hot encoding refers to using a vector, where the number of total elements is equal to the number of classes, of all zeros except the position of the true label is a "1." Table 8.1 demonstrates how the integer labels for this example are converted to one-hot labels. Note that in this example, the integer labels are straightforward to assign since they correspond to the handwritten digit. However, for a different case that does not involve classifying numerical image (e.g., classification of cats, horses, and birds), integer labels can arbitrarily be assigned first to each category and then converted to one hot label.

After preparing the data to fit this form, we will need to select the specific hyperparameters of the MLP. Recall that hyperparameters refer to the characteristics of a machine learning model. In the context of MLPs, hyperparameters refer to the number of layers, and the number of perceptrons in each layer, and could also include other MLP architecture details. The number of perceptrons in the input layer will correspond to the number of input features. Since we are considering an input image with 784 features, we will have 784 perceptrons in the input layer. Similarly, the number of perceptrons in the output layer will correspond to the number of total possible categories (also referred to as classes). For this example, we are trying to classify each image into one of 10 categories (the digits between 0 and 9). Thus, since we have 10 possible classes, the output layer will contain 10 perceptrons. Choosing the number of hidden layers and the number of perceptrons in each hidden layer is less straightforward than choosing the number of perceptrons in the input and output layers. These parameters can be selected much more arbitrarily, and it is also common to compare multiple configurations before selecting a specific architecture. For this application, let us use three hidden layers with the first, second, and third hidden layers containing 64, 128, and 256 perceptrons, respectively.

Next, we need to select the activation functions used in each layer. Although activation functions are applied to each perceptron individually, it is common practice to select activation functions by layer so that each perceptron in a given layer uses the same activation function. Here, let us select common choices of activation functions. That is, we will use the ReLU activation function for each layer except the output layer, which will use the softmax activation function. The softmax activation function is the most common choice of activation function in the output layer of neural networks that are used for classification because they convert the final predictions into probabilities. Thus, the output value of each perceptron in the output layer can be compared and the perceptron with the highest value is the MLP's classification prediction.

Our MLP will operate by taking a grayscale image as input. Specifically, each pixel value of the image will be used as input. Next, the sample will be *forward propagated* through the MLP until it reaches the output. *Forward propagation* refers to the input going through each of the hidden layers and incurring their respective mathematical operations (multiplication by weights, added with bias, and passed through activation function). The classification of the image into one of the ten possible categories will be given by the values produced by the output layer. Specifically, the output of the model will be a 10-element vector corresponding to the 10 perceptrons in the output layer (one element per perceptron). Since we are using the softmax activation function at the output layer, the value of each perceptron in the output layer can be interpreted as the probability of the input belonging to that specific class. So, the value of the first perceptron corresponds to the probability that the input is a "0," the value of the second perceptron corresponds to the probability that the input is a "1," and so on up through the digit "9." The digit corresponding to the element with the maximum probability is the MLP's classification decision for the given input.

Of course, for the MLP to produce accurate predictions, the weights and biases need to be tuned to specific values in order to minimize the error between the true and predicted values. This process occurs during *training*, which will be discussed in Chapter 9.

Convolutional Neural Networks (CNN)

The CNN architecture is the most common deep learning model for visual data processing due to its excellent ability to analyze spatial patterns and correlations. They perform exceptionally well on tasks such as image classification, object detection, and image recognition. The key idea behind CNNs lies in their ability to automatically learn and extract meaningful features from raw input data, such as images. Other common neural networks process images as flat vectors (recall how images were reshaped prior to their input into MLPs), disregarding the spatial relationships between pixels. CNNs, on the other hand, are specifically designed to leverage the spatial structure of inputs.

CNNs consist of a series of mathematical operations that are performed sequentially. Specifically, CNNs consist of a convolutional layer that is often followed by a pooling layer. Large CNNs often have several convolutional and pooling layers, which are then followed by fully connected layers of perceptrons. Let us consider each component of CNN in more detail.

Convolution

Convolution is the mathematical operation at the core of CNNs. It consists of an *input* and a *kernel*. Let us consider the *input* to be an $M \times M$ matrix. This could be, for example, an image as seen by a computer where each entry of the matrix represents the corresponding pixel value of the image (such as an image of a handwritten digit that was discussed earlier with MLPs). A *kernel* is a smaller matrix—in this case, let us consider the kernel to be an $n \times n$ matrix where $n < M$—that is laid over a portion of the input and point-wise multiplied and summed. Then, the kernel is slid over and again point-wise multiplied and summed. This operation continues with the kernel starting in the top left of the input and moving to the right by a certain number of pixels at a time until the kernel is at the top right of the input at which point it slides down by a certain number of pixels and starts again at the left side (similar to reading a page in a book). This continues until the kernel is finally at the bottom right. The number of pixels the kernel is shifted over in each operation is called the *stride*. The output of the convolution here is, thus, also a matrix and referred to as a *feature map*. The convolution operation is described visually in Figure 8.8, and mathematically, we can express convolution as

$$y[j,k] = \sum_{l=1}^{n}\sum_{w=0}^{n} x[j+l, k+w]\, s[l, w]$$

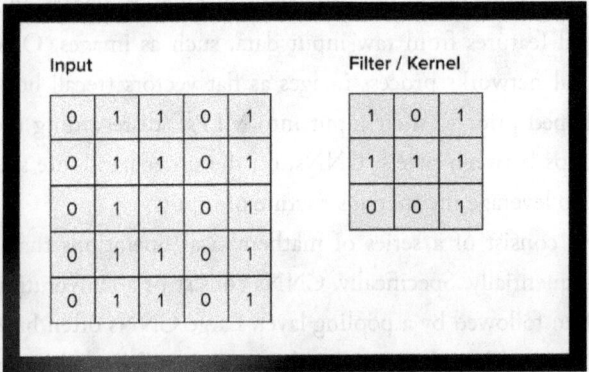

Figure 8.8a Example of an input and kernel used in convolution. Note that both the input and the kernel are different entities. In machine learning, the values of the kernel matrix are updated during the training process of CNN

Image Source: Gavrilova (2021). Convolutional Neural Networks for Beginners.

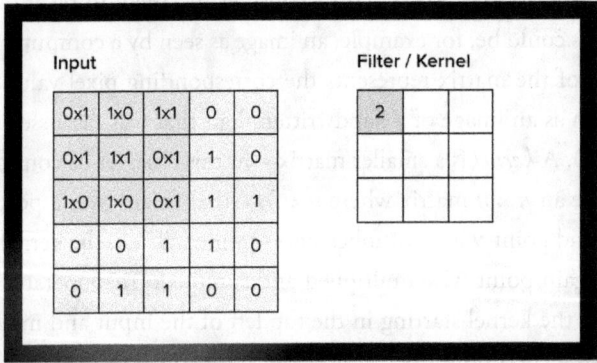

Figure 8.8b Example of how convolution is performed in CNNs between inputs and kernels and a visualization of the convolution equation. The kernel is multiplied point-wise by the input at every position, and the resulting products are summed. This results in the output feature maps

Image Source: Gavrilova, Yulia (2021). Convolutional Neural Networks for Beginners.

where x[j+l,k+w] represents the $j + l$ row and $k + w$ column of the input, $s[l, w]$ represents the lth row and kth column of the kernel, and $y[j, k]$ is the result of the jth row and kth column of the output.

Convolutional Layers

Convolutional layers are the layers that, in large part, comprise CNNs. Convolutional layers consist of several kernels of the same dimension but different parameter values. Thus, a convolutional layer outputs several feature maps, where each feature map corresponds to the output of convolving one kernel with the input. As a result, the number of kernels specified to be in a convolutional layer is equal to the number of feature maps outputted by that layer. Each element of the outputted feature map is then passed through an activation function. Each kernel is initialized to have random values, which are then tuned during the training process. By learning multiple kernels, CNNs become capable of detecting different features at various levels of abstraction, starting from simple edges and textures to more complex structures like shapes and objects. To capture hierarchical patterns, CNNs often stack multiple convolutional layers. Each subsequent layer typically learns to detect higher-level features by combining information from lower-level features learned in previous layers. This hierarchical feature extraction enables CNNs to model complex relationships in visual data more effectively.

Pooling Layers

Pooling layers often, but not always, follow convolutional layers. The pooling layer reduces the dimensions of the feature maps while preserving their essential features. It achieves this by downsampling the feature maps using methods such as max pooling, where the largest value out of each $k \times k$ patch of values in the feature map is kept, or average pooling, where all the values in each $k \times k$ patch is averaged. This downsampling reduces the computational complexity of the network and makes it more robust to small variations and translations in the input data. The pooling process is visualized in Figure 8.9. After several convolutional and pooling layers, the extracted features are usually flattened into a vector and fed into fully

Max Pooling

29	15	28	184
0	100	70	38
12	12	7	2
12	12	45	6

2 x 2
pool size

| 100 | 184 |
| 12 | 45 |

Average Pooling

31	15	28	184
0	100	70	38
12	12	7	2
12	12	45	6

2 x 2
pool size

| 36 | 80 |
| 12 | 15 |

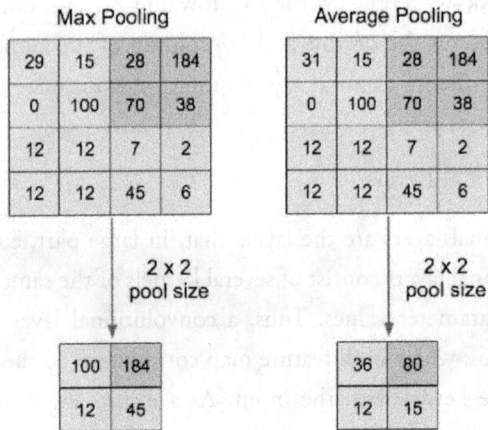

Figure 8.9 Visualization of max pooling and average pooling out of a feature map using a 2 × 2 pooling size

connected layers, which enable the network to make predictions based on the features learned in the convolutional layers.

Example 8.2: Let us revisit *Example 8.1* but this time using CNN as the classification architecture. As we discuss this example, you will notice that we are solving the same classification task as in *Example 8.1* (i.e., designing a classifier to predict the handwritten digit presented in the input image), but we are approaching the problem slightly differently by choosing a different architecture and corresponding hyperparameters.

Let us consider the task of classifying handwritten digits into one of 10 categories (i.e., the digits 0 to 9) as a machine learning task that we would like to construct an MLP to perform. That is, given an image of a handwritten digit, we would like the MLP to predict which digit is between 0 and 9. Images of handwritten digits are shown in Figure 8.5. Each digit is similar but will vary slightly because every human's handwriting is slightly different. Similar to *Example 8.1*, the images shown in Figure 8.6 are digits that may be difficult for a human to read, and we will see that a CNN may similarly face the same problem in classifying them.

We begin by considering each handwritten digit as a low-resolution 28 × 28 grayscale image. In computers, each image is stored as an array of numbers with each value denoting the pixel intensity, which varies between 0 and 255 in integer values. Thus, each image of these handwritten digits is seen by a computer as a 28 × 28 matrix. Unlike with MLPs, we can directly input this matrix into a CNN without having to vertically stack all the features (in this case the features are the pixel values) into a single vector.

Next, we quantitively label the images with their corresponding outputs exactly as shown in Table 8.1. Note that even though this is a CNN, the output layer will still be a fully connected layer with the number of units equal to the number of classes.

After preparing the data to fit this form, we will need to select the specific hyperparameters of the CNN. In the context of CNNs, hyperparameters refer to the number of layers, the number of feature maps in each layer, the kernel size dimensions of each layer, the number of pooling layers, the type of pooling performed at each layer, the activation functions, and where to place the pooling layers in relation to the convolutional layers.

Let us consider a CNN with two convolutional layers and a max pooling subsampling layer following each layer as shown in Figure 8.9. The first and second convolutional layers will have 32 and 64 kernels, respectively. Both convolutional layers will consist of a 5 × 5 dimensional kernel. Both convolutional layers will be followed by a 2 × 2 max pooling subsampling layer, which will select the largest value in each 2 × 2 patch of each feature map. Finally, the output of the last max pooling layer will be flattened into a single vector, which will then be inputted into a fully connected dense layer consisting of 128 units. This layer will then feed into the output layer, which will consist of 10 units (since there are 10 possible classes). Following the same convention used for *Example 8.1*, we will select the ReLU activation functions for each convolutional layer and the fully connected dense layer. At the output, we will apply the softmax activation function so that the outputted predictions can be interpreted as probabilities. After forward propagating an input through the CNN, the values of the output layer can be used to predict the model's predictions exactly as done in *Example 8.1* (and all other neural networks used for classification).

Like the MLP from *Example 8.1*, the CNN's kernel values (weights) and fully connected layer parameters (weights and biases) need to be tuned to specific values in order to minimize the error between the true and predicted values. This *training* process will be discussed in Chapter 9.

Other Common Neural Network Architectures

In addition to MLPs and CNNs, a variety of other neural network architectures have been developed for different types of data. One of the most prevalent of these architectures is the RNN. RNNs are designed to operate most effectively on time-series data (e.g., a data stream read at sequential time stamps from a sensor). Unlike traditional feedforward models such as MLPs and CNNs, recurrent layers in RNNs have multiple outputs. Some of these outputs are recursively fed back into the recurrent layer and used to calculate the output. RNNs also have a variety of derivatives such as long short-term memory cells, gated recurrent units (GRUs), and transformers. These derivatives have been adopted in ubiquitous machine learning applications, which will be further discussed in Chapter 10.

In addition, several other neural network architectures exist such as restricted Boltzmann machines, Hopfield networks, and deep belief networks. Although an in-depth study of each of these different types of architectures is outside the scope of this text, it is important to note that architectures other than the ones discussed here exist. They are deployed similarly to the MLP and CNN architectures discussed throughout this chapter, but they differ in the mathematical operations they perform, the sequence in which they are performed, and, to some extent, their specific training methods.

Key Takeaways and Summary

In this chapter, we discussed deep learning models, which are among the most common machine learning models. We began by discussing the fundamentals of deep learning, which are neural networks, and we discussed the foundational operations of these networks including perceptrons, and activation functions. We then discussed two specific types of neural network architectures in-depth: the MLP and the CNN. We dove into specific examples with each architecture and examined the different components of each model. Finally, we gave a very brief overview of other types of architecture that exist.

PART 4

Training Machine Learning Models

CHAPTER 9

Training Machine Learning Models

Chapter Highlights

- Choosing a Model
  - Guidelines for Model Selection
- Model Training
  - Hyperparameter Tuning
- Model Evaluation
  - Overfitting and Underfitting

Up till now, we have explored the foundational concepts of machine learning including its key elements, data preparation, simple supervised and unsupervised models, classification and regression tasks, and deep learning. We will now turn to one of the most crucial aspects of machine learning: model training and tuning. This is the process during which the numerical values of the selected machine learning model are calculated and optimized to maximize performance. The performance measure will utilize a specific metric (e.g., accuracy, precision, mean squared error (MSE), etc.) depending on the task the model is being trained to perform (e.g., classification or regression). We will discuss how the aforementioned performance is measured for varying tasks throughout this chapter and they can be used to compare different models that are being considered.

We will begin by discussing how to choose a model. Up till now, we have discussed several different types of problems that machine learning can solve as well as a variety of different machine learning models. Here, we will aggregate these ideas to form a foundational understanding of which models are appropriate for certain tasks.

With the chosen model in hand, we will move to discuss the core principle of this chapter—model training. Here, we will discuss different mathematical tools, such as loss functions and optimization algorithms, that are used to quantify and assess the model training performance. This discussion will be kept broad and applicable to all machine learning models. The objective is to give an overview of the model training pipeline used in machine learning rather than delve into the details and differences of training-specific models.

Throughout the discussion of model training, we will also discuss the notion of hyperparameter tuning. Hyperparameters refer to the values chosen for a specific model (e.g., number of input features, number of coefficients in a regression, and number of layers in a neural network). These values are selected by the data scientist implementing the model and, while general guidelines exist for choosing a hyperparameter architecture, they often need to be adjusted after assessing the initial model's performance. The process of adjusting these values is known as hyperparameter tuning, and we will discuss this when training is discussed.

Finally, after training a machine learning model and performing hyperparameter tuning, we will discuss how to evaluate the performance of the trained model. Very frequently, machine learning practitioners will consider a variety of models to implement for a given task. Therefore, standard metrics must exist so that different models can be compared with as much consistency as possible. We will discuss how to evaluate and compare such models and assess the tradeoffs that should be examined when selecting the ultimate model for the given task. We will also discuss the notion of overfitting and underfitting to a data set. These are common problems that are encountered when training machine learning models, and we will discuss methods to mitigate these issues.

Choosing a Model

Let us begin by discussing how to choose a model. Selecting the correct model to deploy is a crucial decision in the machine learning pipeline. As we have seen up till now, a large number of machine learning models exist, and each model is suitable for different types of problems and data. Therefore, we must first identify the type of problem that is aiming to be solved. From this point, we can narrow down a list of models that effectively solve that problem. At this point, we can compare the narrowed-down list of models that may work for the selected problem. It is not vital to have a single model selected at this stage but rather a list of candidate models that can be compared during the model evaluation phase of training.

To begin identifying the type of problem, we first consider whether we will be using supervised or unsupervised learning.

- **Supervised learning**: in supervised learning, the data set is labeled. This means that the data set contains input data along with corresponding output labels or target values. In supervised learning, the objective is to train the model to map inputs to outputs, enabling it to make accurate predictions on new and unseen data. If the machine learning problem will use supervised learning, we must next identify if the problem will be a classification or regression problem.
  - *Classification*: in classification, the model assigns input data to predefined classes or categories. This includes binary classification, where we are aiming to identify the input into one of two categories (e.g., is the email *spam* or *not spam* or is the picture a *cat* or a *dog*), and multivariate classification, where we are aiming to identify the input into one of three or more categories (e.g., is the image a *cat*, *dog*, or *mouse*). If the data set encompasses a classification problem, consider applying the following machine learning models (which have been discussed in-depth in the preceding chapters):
    - Logistic regression (for binary classification only)
    - Support vector machine (for binary classification only)
    - Linear discriminant analysis (for binary classification only)
    - Naïve bayes classifiers (for binary and multivariate classification)
    - K-nearest neighbor (for binary and multivariate classification)

- Random forest (for binary and multivariate classification)
- Deep learning models including MLPs and CNNs (for binary and multivariate classification)
  - *Regression*: regression deals with predicting continuous numerical values. For example, forecasting house prices based on square footage and number of bedrooms or forecasting diamond prices based on its size and karat are regression tasks. If the data set encompasses a regression task, consider applying the following machine learning models (which have been discussed in-depth in the preceding chapters):
    - Linear regression
    - Nonlinear regression
    - Ridge regression
    - Decision trees and random forests (these models can also be used for regression tasks by predicting numerical values instead of classes)
    - Deep learning models including MLPs and CNNs (these models can also be used for regression tasks by predicting numerical values instead of classes)
- **Unsupervised learning**: in unsupervised learning, the data set is not labeled. This means that the data set contains input data along with no corresponding output labels or target values. One of the most common unsupervised learning problems is clustering, where, as discussed previously, we aim to group similar types of data based on different characteristics (the exact characteristics that are prioritized during clustering differ depending on the model that's used). Moreover, we never begin with or have access to any ground truth labels, so we assess these models differently than classification models. Unsupervised learning approaches include:
  - K-means
  - Mixture models
  - Deep learning models including MLPs and CNNs (these models can be used to transform the data into other representations, i.e., perform feature engineering)

In addition to identifying the type of problem, other characteristics should also be considered when choosing the model to train on a given data set. These include data characteristics, model interpretability, and computational resources. For example, if the data set is small, we may want to avoid using a model that is computationally intensive to train such as a neural network. A variety of factors can be considered when selecting a model and it is most important to select a model that strikes a good balance between solving the machine learning problem effectively and addressing other design and data constraints. With one or more candidate models selected, we can turn to the training phase of the selected model(s).

Model Training

After obtaining a prepared data set and selecting a model (or list of candidate models), we are ready to begin the model training process. Training a machine learning model refers to adjusting the model's parameters to minimize the differences between its predictions and the ground truth target values. This process is also called *learning* because the model parameters are updated based on the patterns it observes during training.

Prior to the start of training the complete data set is split into a training set, a validation set, and a testing set. The training set is used to tune the parameter values of the model and perform the actual training. The validation set is used to ensure that the model is learning effectively on data that is not being used to directly train the model. These two data sets are used to train the model and achieve desirable performance on the validation set. Finally, the testing set is used to perform model evaluation. The metrics that are measured to evaluate the model are calculated using the samples in the testing set. If multiple models are being compared, the same samples are kept in each of the three data sets for consistency. It is common to use about 70 percent of the available data for training, about 15 percent of the available data for validation, and about 15 percent of the available data for testing. Each set should be disjoint and, hence, no samples should be in more than one of the data sets.

Although training any machine learning model refers to adjusting its parameters to reduce the error between its predictions and ground truth value, each machine learning model is trained slightly differently since each model behaves differently. Several models, such as non-deep learning-based regression models and naïve Bayes classification, have a closed-form training method (i.e., a mathematical formula exists that the data can be plugged into to determine the model parameter values) such as least squares or Bayes' theorem. However, other models, such as logistic regression and ubiquitous deep learning models, are trained iteratively. The overarching iterative training process is outlined below.

1. Initialization: the process of assigning parameter values at the beginning of training is called initialization. These parameter values will be adjusted during the training process. After the model is selected, initial parameter values are required and it is often not desirable to set them to all 0's, 1's, or a combination. Instead, the initial model parameters should be chosen randomly. It is common practice to assign the initial values from a probability distribution, but this is not required. Model parameters can also be initialized using the parameter values of another machine learning model that has already been trained. This is known as *transfer learning* and is known to help reduce the number of training iterations required.

2. Forward pass: using the current model parameter values and training data set, the data are passed through the model to make predictions. The output predictions are then compared to the actual target values.

3. Loss computation: a loss function is used to compute the error between the model's predictions and the ground truth values (a more detailed discussion of loss functions is presented below). In this training stage, the loss (error) is computed on the training set and the validation set. Since the validation set is not used directly to update the model parameters over iterations, it provides an unbiased metric indicating if the model is learning. Specifically, a decrease in both the validation loss (the loss computed on the validation set) and training loss (the loss computed on the training set) should be observed to indicate that the model is learning. This should occur naturally because as the model learns, its loss (error) should decrease. Similarly, if the loss (error) does not decrease over iterations, the model is not learning and therefore not being trained properly.

4. Backward pass: the objective of measuring the loss in Step 3 is to minimize it. Naturally, by minimizing the loss, the performance and accuracy of the model should increase. The next step in the training process is to do exactly that via the backward pass. In this stage, an optimization algorithm (usually *gradient descent*) is deployed which calculates the loss (from Step 3) with respect to each parameter in the model. In other words, during the backward pass, the error contributed by each parameter value to the total loss is calculated. Note that the backward pass is only computed on the training set. The validation set is used only to calculate the overall loss at the end of a forward pass to observe the model's behavior on data that are not directly used to update the model parameters.

5. Parameter update: using the values obtained in Step 4 in which the error contribution from each parameter value was found, the parameter values of the model are updated accordingly to decrease the overall loss.

6. Repeat: Steps 2 to 5 are repeated for a certain number of iterations (training iterations are commonly called *epochs*) that are predefined by the data scientist. Other stopping criteria can also be applied. For example, after several iterations, the loss may only decrease by a nominal amount and not contribute to the training process. Thus, one stopping criterion could be to stop the training process before the predefined number of epochs if the loss stops decreasing by smaller than a certain amount. Criteria such as this that terminate the training process before the predefined number of epochs are called early stopping.

During the training process, we must also effectively handle hyperparameters, which are settings chosen by the data scientist that govern the learning process but are not learned from the data. For example, the number of layers in a neural network, the number of units in a layer, and the number of epochs are all hyperparameters. Tuning the hyperparameters is critical as they can directly affect the model's performance on specific tasks. No exact rules or theoretical constructs exist to guide hyperparameter tuning, but some guidelines are known to be effective. For example, when training a Convolutional Neural Netwrk (CNN), it is highly encouraged to select an architecture that is known to work on another data set that may be similar to the one at hand. Hyperparameter tuning is usually performed at the end of the training process outlined in Steps 1 to 6 above. Then, the model is retrained to assess if the updated hyperparameters improved the training process.

In addition to splitting the data into a training, validation, and testing set once and evaluating performance, it is common (and also good practice) to use cross validation to mitigate biases in the evaluated metrics due to the data set splits. Cross validation divides the data into multiple train/validation/test splits and trains and evaluates the model multiple times. The model is evaluated on each testing set and the resulting metrics from each fold are averaged. k-fold cross validation is a common cross-validation technique, which splits the data k times.

After performing model training, hyperparameter turning, and cross validation using the training and validation set, and arriving at a desirable training and validation loss value, the model is considered trained, and its evaluation can begin.

Model Evaluation

Now that one or more candidate models have been trained, it is time to discuss model evaluation, which assesses and quantifies the model's performance to generalize on new, unseen data. The primary purpose of model evaluation is to determine its performance on real-world data as well as to detect any inherent problems that might have occurred during the training process. Model evaluation also provides us with a set of numerical metrics that can be used to compare multiple models, on the same data, and select the strongest one.

Several different metrics exist to quantify model performance on supervised learning tasks. Typically, the metric to use depends on whether a classification or regression task was used. Below are some common evaluation metrics used in supervised learning. It is indicated whether the metric is used for classification and/or regression tasks. Notice that each metric relies on quantitatively comparing the predicted labels of the testing set from the model to the ground truth labels. In other words, each performance metric uses both the predicted and true labels to formulate a useful metric.

- Accuracy (for binary and multivariate classification): the ratio of correctly predicted samples to the total number of samples. This is usually either represented as a decimal between 0 and 1 or as a percentage between 0 and 100. Use caution to express accuracy consistently.
- Confusion matrix (for binary and multivariate classification): a confusion matrix does not produce a single metric, but rather it allows for the visualization of each prediction and whether it corresponds to the actual ground truth class. A sample confusion matrix is visualized in Figure 9.1.
- Precision (for binary classification): the ratio between the proportion of true positive predictions to all positive predictions. This is also usually expressed as a decimal between 0 and 1 or as a percentage between 0 and 100. This is important when mitigating false positives is prioritized (e.g., false positive detection incurs high costs).
- Recall (for binary classification): the ratio between true positive predictions and all positive predictions. Again, this is usually expressed as a decimal between 0 and 1 or as a percentage between 0 and 100. Recall is an important metric to consider when mitigating false negative predictions is prioritized.
- Area Under ROC Curve (AUC) (for binary classification): the AUC quantifies the ability of a binary classifier to distinguish between two classes. It is desirable when the data set is imbalanced (i.e., the data set has significantly more samples corresponding to one class than the other). The AUC ranges between 0 and 1. A value close to 1 indicates that the model is able to accurately distinguish between classes, a value close to 0 indicates that the model consistently confuses the two labels for one another, and a value close to 0.5 indicates that the model cannot distinguish between classes.
- MSE (regression): the average of the squared differences between the predicted and true values. MSE is a very commonly used metric, but it is very sensitive to outliers (in this case, outliers are predicted samples that deviate

Confusion Matrix

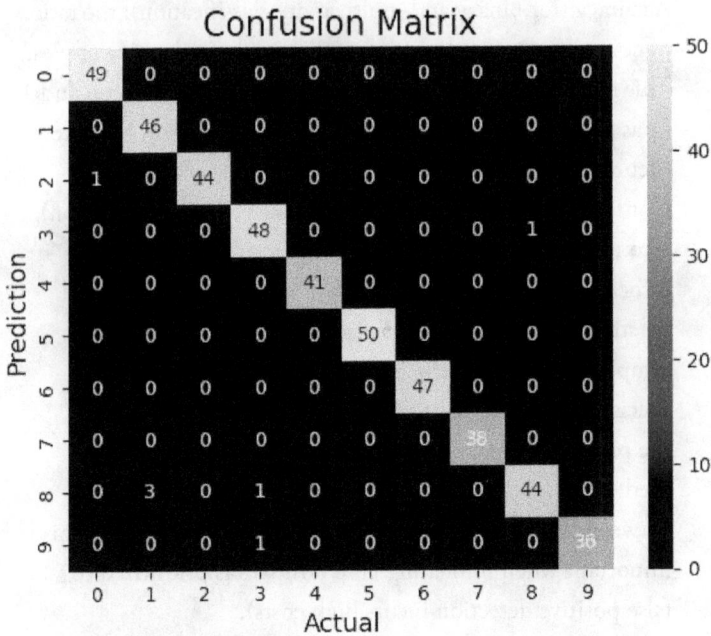

Figure 9.1 A sample confusion matrix visualization. The x-axis represents the true labels, and the y-axis represents the predicted labels from the model. The numbers in the matrix are the number of samples that correspond to that prediction scenario. Confusion matrices are often color coded, such as the one shown here, to emphasize where the highest volumes of predictions are located in the matrix

significantly from the true output). There is no specific range that the MSE falls between, but it is always greater than or equal to 0. The range of the MSE depends on the scale of the outputs and predicted values.

- Mean Absolute Error (MAE) (regression): the average of the absolute differences between the predicted and true values. MAE is a less commonly used metric, and it is less sensitive to outliers compared to MSE. Similar to the MSE, there is no specific range that the MAE falls between, but it is always greater than or equal to 0. Again, the range of the MAE depends on the scale of the outputs and predicted values.

- Coefficient of determination (R2 value) (regression): the coefficient of determination measures the proportion of the variance in the model's predictions that are predicted by the model. This is a value between 0 and 1 that essentially measures how well the model makes predictions. A value closer to 1 indicates a good ability of the model to make predictions, whereas a value closer to 0 indicates an inability of the model to make accurate predictions.

As discussed above, several metrics exist to assess the model performance of supervised machine learning models, and the choice of evaluation metric depends on the specific machine learning task being performed and the characteristics of the data. However, it is often good practice to use a combination of these metrics to perform model evaluation and select the most suitable model because one metric alone may be misleading. For example, if we are working on a binary classification task with a test set that contains 1,000 samples of which 950 samples belong to the nontarget class and 50 samples belong to the other target class, a model could predict each sample as being a nontarget with an accuracy of 95.5 percent. Although the accuracy would be high, the model is unable to distinguish the two classes and thus would not be very effective during deployment. In this case, we would also want to consider using the AUC score since it would account for the imbalance in the testing set and result in a value of 0.5 if each sample was predicted to be in one of the two classes.

All the metrics discussed above are applicable to supervised learning only. As discussed throughout this section, a lot of choices are available to use when evaluating supervised machine learning models. Evaluating the performance of unsupervised models, however, can be more challenging since no ground truth labels are typically available to compare against. Nevertheless, a handful of evaluation techniques can be used to perform model evaluation on unsupervised models. They are not very commonly used, however, and the decision to use them varies drastically between applications and models. Therefore, we will not discuss specific examples of evaluation metrics for unsupervised models as it is outside the scope of general model evaluation commonly used in machine learning.

Lastly, let us discuss two very common behaviors that all machine learning models are known to display: overfitting and underfitting. Both of these terms refer to the model not being able to properly generalize to unseen data and thus behave poorly during model evaluation. *Overfitting* in machine learning occurs when a model performs very well on a training set (e.g., very high accuracy and very low loss) but performs very poorly on a testing set (e.g., very low accuracy and high loss). Overfitting indicates a lack of the model's ability to generalize to unseen data. This typically happens when there are too many differences between the samples in the training and testing set (sometimes due to a nonrandom data split) and, as a result, the model merely memorizes the training data without regard to generalizability. To combat overfitting, techniques like regularization, cross validation, and more diverse splits to training and testing data can be employed to encourage models to generalize better and avoid memorization. *Underfitting*, on the other hand, refers to a situation where a model is unable to capture the underlying patterns in the data, resulting in poor training and testing performance. Underfitting is usually due to a model not being complex enough to capture the patterns in the data that is trying to be learned. It can be addressed by using a more complex model (e.g., using a neural network instead of a support vector machine) and adding more parameters to a model (e.g., more layers in a neural network) so that the additional parameters are better able to learn the data.

Key Takeaways and Summary

In this chapter, we discussed a general overview of how model training is performed in machine learning models. We began with guidelines on choosing a particular model by asking questions about the data at hand and the type of problem that was aiming to be solved. Next, we discussed the overall training process in which the model parameters are updated to minimize the error between its predictions and ground truth output. Finally, we discussed the model evaluation process, where we introduced common metrics used to assess and compare the performance of different machine learning models. Ultimately, this pipeline will lead to developing accurate and robust models for deployment.

PART 5

Current State of Machine Learning

CHAPTER 10

Real-World Applications of Machine Learning

Chapter Highlights

- Introduction
- ML in Health Care
- Natural Language Processing
- Autonomous Vehicles
- Recommender Systems

Introduction

Up until now, we have explored various technical approaches to machine learning (ML). In this context, we have seen different ML models, training methods, and data preparation techniques. We have also seen small-scale applications of ML used for solving specific types of problems in various domains. Now, in this chapter, we will turn our attention to the broader use cases of ML as they are applied in a variety of domains and industries. Although ML is being increasingly applied in several domains, this chapter will focus on the domains that are seeing the greatest potential benefits and research activity from ML. In this chapter, we will focus on ML application in four domains: (i) ML in health care, (ii) natural language processing (NLP), (iii) autonomous vehicles, and (iv) recommender systems. In each domain, we will discuss the state-of-the-art as well as current limitations and challenges faced by each specific domain in the context of applying ML to it.

ML in Health Care

The health care domain has been transforming into a field that produces vast amounts of data from a range of sources such as imaging, lab results, and electronic health records (EHR). The need to draw conclusions about a patient's health paired with the vast amounts of produced data led to the natural application of ML in health care. Although health care is a vast field, making the potential applications of ML in health care equally vast, we will focus on one of the key usages of ML in health care: early disease detection.

The most prominent clinical application of ML has been in the early detection and (human-aided) diagnoses of diseases by localizing and classifying abnormalities on medical images, particularly in the early stages when they are difficult for humans (including trained professionals) to detect with the naked eye. Such medical imaging scans include, but are not limited to, medical resonance imaging (MRI), computed tomography (CT) scans, and x-rays. In this capacity, convolutional neural networks (CNNs) have been utilized to automatically segment cartilage and assess osteoarthritis risk in MRIs of the knee, outperforming manual non-ML approaches. Additionally, deep learning has been applied for segmenting multiple sclerosis lesions in 3D MRI scans as well as for differentially diagnosing benign and malignant breast nodules from ultrasound images. CNNs also matched the performance of dermatologists in classifying biopsy-proven clinical images of various skin cancers, including keratinocyte carcinomas and malignant melanomas, across a vast data set of 130,000 images. This underscores the transformative potential of deep learning in enhancing medical image analysis and diagnosis accuracy.

In addition, several studies have applied deep learning to predict diseases from a patient's clinical status shown in their EHRs. For example, CNNs have been used to predict congestive heart failure and chronic obstructive pulmonary disease, demonstrating significant advantages over baseline methods. Recurrent neural networks (RNNs) have been used on word embeddings to infer current illness states and predict future outcomes, incorporating medical interventions for dynamic predictions. RNNs have also been used for predicting diagnoses and medications based on patient history, showcasing higher recall than non-deep learning-based baselines. Deep learning was also applied to model continuous time signals, such as laboratory results, for automatic phenotype identification. Additionally, natural language models (which will be discussed in more detail below) were employed to learn embedded representations of medical concepts from EHRs, demonstrating applications in predicting suicide risk and de-identifying clinical notes. Notably, the prediction of unplanned patient readmissions after discharge has received attention, with one study showing that CNNs can accurately predict readmissions within six months. The use of predictive models such as CNNs helps with early intervention, where such readmissions can be avoided when detected early enough.

Despite these exciting advancements, ML incurs several limitations in its applications to health care. Its primary challenge revolves around trust and accuracy. Current state-of-the-art ML models in health care still make mistakes, and in the context of health care, mistakes made by an ML model can lead to incorrect diagnoses among a host of other problems. This challenge largely stems from the lack of medical data volume compared to other domains. Health data's heterogeneity, temporality, and complexity present hurdles for training effective models leading to less generalizable models. Existing deep learning models often assume static inputs, neglecting the evolving nature of diseases over time. Moreover, the interpretability of deep learning models in health care is crucial for gaining medical professionals' trust. Despite these challenges, opportunities for future research include feature enrichment by capturing diverse patient data sources, federated inference to maintain data privacy across clinical institutions so that data do not have to be physically transmitted, and addressing model privacy concerns through differential privacy standards. Incorporating expert knowledge, temporal modeling, and developing interpretable modeling methods are essential directions for enhancing the effectiveness and trustworthiness of ML in health care.

Natural Language Processing

The field of NLP is primarily devoted to increasing computers' understanding of human language in both spoken and written forms. Digital voice assistants on mobile phones as well as large language models (LLMs) are both prominent examples of ML-powered NLP.

The majority of NLP algorithms are based on transformers, which are a class of neural network architectures like CNNs and RNNs. Recently, generative pretrained transformers (GPT) have received a lot of attention due to their impressive ability to learn from large volumes of text and then generate unique responses based on various prompts. This has been the most prolific with OpenAI's ChatGPT, which is an LLM designed to understand and generate human-like text using patterns and information obtained during training consisting of various pieces of text on the internet. At its core, LLMs including ChatGPT are ML models trained according to the same pipeline we have seen throughout this text. For example, when GPT-3.5 was prompted with "How do you work?," it responded with the following:

I am a machine learning model called GPT-3.5, developed by OpenAI. My architecture is known as the "Generative Pre-trained Transformer 3.5." Here's a simplified explanation of how I work:

1. ***Pretraining***: *I've been trained on a diverse range of internet text up until my knowledge cutoff date in January 2022. This pretraining involves predicting what comes next in a sentence, given the context of the previous words. This process helps me learn grammar, facts, reasoning abilities, and some level of world knowledge.*
2. ***Architecture***: *I am based on a transformer architecture, which is a type of neural network architecture. Transformers are known for their ability to process and generate human-like text by attending to different parts of a sequence of words.*
3. ***Fine-tuning***: *While I'm not fine-tuned to specific tasks or data sets, my general architecture can be adapted for different applications by fine-tuning on specific data. However, in public usage, I don't have access to information about specific individuals unless it has been shared with me in the course of our conversation.*
4. ***Natural Language Understanding***: *I can understand and generate human-like text, making me versatile in various language-related tasks, such as answering questions, generating creative content, translating languages, and more.*
5. ***Limitations***: *Despite my capabilities, I have limitations. I might generate incorrect or nonsensical answers, be sensitive to the input phrasing,*

and lack a true understanding of context. I don't have personal experiences, emotions, or consciousness. My responses are generated based on patterns learned during training.

In summary, I work by using patterns and information learned during my training to generate human-like text based on the input I receive. My purpose is to assist and provide information to the best of my ability.

As we can see from its own response above, LLMs are trained using the same ML pipeline that we have seen multiple times throughout this text. The specifics of the training, of course, differ between models but the overarching approach, in terms of architecture selection, data collection, model training, and so on, is the same as it is for any ML model.

Autonomous Vehicles

The integration of ML into autonomous vehicles is a highly researched area as it has the potential for a wide range of civilian and military applications. Beyond the familiar realm of self-driving cars, ML algorithms are instrumental in enabling various autonomous vehicles, including unmanned aerial systems (UAS), maritime vessels, and delivery robots, to perceive their surroundings, make decisions, and navigate dynamically. Here, we will discuss the applications and limitations of ML in autonomous vehicles in a variety of fields.

The most prevalent application of ML in autonomous vehicles is for self-driving cars. Such vehicles employ an array of sensors, cameras, and lidar to perceive their environment, with ML algorithms processing the data collected from these sensors in real time. Deep learning models are usually trained offline on a collection of real-world and simulated data. During deployment, models can also be actively trained. The changes incurred from online training could be local to a particular vehicle's software, or they could be reflected in all vehicles through a software update.

UASs are becoming a more prominent application for leveraging the autonomy provided by ML algorithms for various tasks including obstacle avoidance, navigation, and route planning. As these vehicles traverse dynamic environments, ML algorithms analyze sensor data to adapt to changes, avoid collisions, and optimize their flight paths. For example, in agriculture, UASs equipped with ML algorithms can assess crop health, identify pests, and optimize irrigation based on real-time data by flying around farms, taking pictures with an onboard camera, and processing them locally on the UAS with results being sent directly to appropriate personnel. ML algorithms for such applications work very similarly as they do for self-driving cars. Specifically, data are collected and deep learning models are first trained offline. Then, models are deployed on the UAS for the online processing of data.

Autonomous ships and underwater vehicles also employ ML for navigation, collision avoidance, and path planning. Equipped with sensors such as sonar and radar, these vessels utilize deep learning algorithms to navigate the complexities of maritime environments in a similar fashion to their usage in other autonomous vehicles. Maritime applications are still an emerging area, but they have promise for both civilian and military purposes.

Currently, the ubiquitous deployment of ML on fleets of autonomous vehicles is limited by two main factors. First, the collected data are often not representative of the environments the autonomous vehicle will encounter. For example, consider the problem of deploying an ML system for a fleet of ships for navigation. The objective of the model is to perform object detection by processing images from the vessel to avoid collisions. In order to do this, data would be collected from existing surface vessels to create a training set. However, if data were only collected during the day when the weather was clear, the model would have poor performance during the night and/or in snowy weather. One solution to this problem could be to collect data in these conditions. However, we are restricted to data collection on the days the vessels are actually in-movement. This would ultimately lead to a nonrepresentative data set. Second, transmitting data collected on multiple participating autonomous agents may not be feasible due to security risks. For example, if navigation data is being actively collected, it may be risky to transmit that data in real time. One method, known as federated learning (FL), has emerged in an attempt to remedy this problem. FL allows for ML models to be trained in a distributed manner and only requires model parameters to be transmitted rather than data itself. Although FL is a promising solution toward privacy-preserving ML, it is still susceptible to malicious attacks in which the transmitted parameters can be intercepted and reverse engineered to recover the training data. Current research is aimed at directly addressing these types of limitations in an effort to move toward the deployment of robust and secure ML systems in autonomous vehicles.

Recommender Systems

Recommendation systems are a type of information-filtering system that provides suggestions for items that are most pertinent to a particular user. For example, new connection requests recommended on social media platforms, merchandise recommended for users based on their previous purchases on online shopping websites, and titles suggested for users to watch provided by streaming services are all examples of ML-powered recommendation systems. User engagement and content consumption have experienced transformative advancements in personalization due to the integration of ML into recommendation systems. These systems, designed to provide user-specific suggestions, leverage ML algorithms to analyze user behavior and preferences. Here, we will explore the intricacies of how ML is harnessed in recommendation systems. Let us begin by examining the different types of ML-based recommendation systems.

In the realm of recommendation systems, collaborative filtering stands out as a prominent approach. This technique relies on users' interactions with available items as the foundation for generating recommendations. It can be implemented in two forms: user-based collaborative filtering, which compares a user's preferences with those of similar users, and item-based collaborative filtering, which suggests items based on their similarity to those previously liked by the user. This is often used by streaming services to recommend certain titles and videos to a user.

Content-based filtering, another type of ML-based recommendation system, takes a different route by recommending items based on the features intrinsic to those items. NLP techniques often play a crucial role in extracting relevant features from textual data. For example, music may be recommended based on the titles that are typically listened to.

Matrix factorization, a more nuanced technique, involves breaking down user-item interaction matrices into labels that represent underlying characteristics. Linear algebra approaches such as singular value decomposition (SVD) and alternating least squares (ALS) are commonly used in matrix factorization. Matrix factorization is often used to recommend products based on user purchase history and preferences.

Training an ML model for recommendation systems commences with data collection and preprocessing. These systems are usually trained on extensive user data, including preferences, interactions, and contextual information. Rigorous preprocessing is required to clean and transform data into a suitable format for training.

Feature engineering plays a pivotal role in refining the model's performance. Depending on the recommendation system type, relevant data attributes are selected and transformed. For collaborative filtering, this may involve user preferences, while content-based systems might focus on item features. The features used to train recommendation systems are usually unique to the context for which the system is being developed.

Model training, a critical phase, can take the form of supervised or unsupervised learning approaches, depending on the recommendation system's nature. Algorithms such as k-nearest neighbors (k-NN), support vector machines (SVM), and neural networks are commonly employed. Deep learning models have also gained traction for their ability to capture intricate patterns in user behavior.

Despite the advancements facilitated by ML in recommendation systems, certain limitations persist. The cold start problem poses a considerable challenge, particularly when dealing with new users or items lacking sufficient interaction data. The cold start problem refers to systems not having any user data prior to their usage of the platform. Data sparsity further complicates the accuracy of recommendations, especially when users have limited interactions with items. Matrix factorization techniques may exacerbate this issue as they rely on complete user–item interaction matrices. Overfitting, a common concern in ML, can lead to overly specific recommendations tailored to individual user preferences, resulting in poor generalization to new users or items. Mitigating strategies such as regularization techniques and careful model tuning are essential to address this challenge. Thus, despite the exciting strides made in ML-based recommendation systems, several challenges still present themselves and are the focus of current research in the field.

Closing Remarks

Throughout this text, we have seen an introduction to current ML approaches. This has included data collection and processing, appropriate methods for data splitting, various types of ML using a wide range of models, model evaluation metrics, deep learning approaches, and applications of ML in different real-world contexts. Several of the concepts that are commonly used in ML are not new and were developed several decades ago (e.g., the idea of artificial neural networks was developed in the mid-1900s). However, the development of more capable computers paired with the plethora of data that has been produced by digital computers and sensors over the recent decades has accelerated the advancements of ML. Although ML has matured quite a bit, as we saw throughout this text, it still faces several challenges that must be addressed before ML can be widely adopted. The next few decades are expected to be more toward secure, reliable, and robust ML.

Bibliography

1. Donoho, David "50 Years of Data Science." *Journal of Computational and Graphical Statistics* **26** no. 4 (2017): 745–766. doi:10.1080/10618600.2017.1384734. S2CID 114558008.

2. Grimes, Seth. "Unstructured Data and the 80 Percent Rule." *Breakthrough Analysis—Bridgepoints,* Clarabridge, August 1, 2008. https://assets.techrepublic.com/uploads/2017/07/07-17-Unstructured-Data-SPG.MP4

3. https://en.wikipedia.org/wiki/Data_science#cite_note-Hayashi-3.

4. "EMC News Press Release: New Digital Universe Study Reveals Big Data Gap: Less Than 1% of World's Data Is Analyzed; Less Than 20% is Protected." *EMC Corporation,* December 2012. www.emc.com.

5. Mike, Koby; Hazzan, Orit. "What is Data Science?" *Communications of the ACM* **66** no. 2 (August 20, 2023): 12–13. https://doi.org/10.1145/357566. ISSN 0001-0782.

6. Hayashi, Chikio. "What Is Data Science ? Fundamental Concepts and a Heuristic Example." Data Science, Classification, and Related Methods. Studies in Classification, Data Analysis, and Knowledge Organization. Springer Japan (January 1, 1998): 40–51. https://link.springer.com/chapter/10.1007/978-4-431-65950-1_3. ISBN 9784431702085.

7. Cao, Longbing. "Data Science: A Comprehensive Overview." *ACM Computing Surveys* 50, no. 3 (June 29, 2017): 43:1–43:42. https://doi.org/10.1145/30762. ISSN 0360-0300. S2CID 207595944.

8. Borchers, Callum. "Behind the Scenes of the 'Sexiest Job of the 21st Century'." *Boston Globe,* November 11, 2015. www.bostonglobe.com/business/2015/11/11/behind-scenes-sexiest-job-century/Kc1cvXIu31DfH-hVmyRQeIJ/story.html.

9. Davenport, Thomas. "Is Data Scientist Still the Sexiest Job of the 21st Century?" *Harvard Business Review,* July 15, 2022. https://hbr.org/2022/07/is-data-scientist-still-the-sexiest-job-of-the-21st-century.

10. Chambers, John. M "Greater or Lesser Statistics: A Choice for Future Research." *Statistics and Computing* 3, no. 4 (December 1, 1993): 182–184. https://doi.org/10.1007/BF00141776. ISSN 0960-3174

11. Wu, C. F.J. PDF. "Statistics=Data Science?" Accessed April 2, 2020. www2. isye.gatech.edu/~jeffwu/presentations/datascien%20ce.pdf.

12. Dhar, Vasant. "Data Science and Prediction." *Communications of the ACM*. 56, no. 12 (December 1, 2013): 64–73. https://doi.org/ 10.1145/250049. S2CID 6107147.

13. Statmodeling.stat.columbia.edu. "Statistics is the least important part of data science « Statistical Modeling, Causal Inference, and Social Science." Accessed April 3, 2020. https://statmodeling.stat.columbia. edu/2013/11/14/statistics-least-important-part-data-science/.

14. Zhou, Victor. "Machine Learning for Beginners: An Introduction to Neural Networks." *Medium*, December 20, 2019. https://towards datascience.com/machine-learning-for-beginners-an-introduction-to-neu-ral-networks-d49f22d238f9.

15. IBM. "What Is Machine Learning?" Accessed June 27, 2023. www.ibm. com/think/sustainability.

16. https://en.wikipedia.org/wiki/Training,_validation,_and_test_data _sets#training_set

17. Alpaydin, Ethem. *Introduction to Machine Learning*, 4th ed. (MIT, 2020). xix, 1–3, 13–18. ISBN 978-0262043793.

18. https://en.wikipedia.org/wiki/Machine_learning#cite_note-islr-30.

19. https://en.wikipedia.org/wiki/Artificial_intelligence#cite_note-FOOTNO-TEGoogle2016

20. Russell, Stuart, J. and Peter, Norvig. *Artificial Intelligence: A Modern Approach* 3rd ed. (Prentice Hall, 2010). ISBN 9780136042594.

21. Freund, Y. and R.E. Schapire. "Large Margin Classification Using the Perceptron Algorithm." *Machine Learning* 37, no. 3 (1999): 277–296. https:// doi.org/10.1023/A:1007662407062. S2CID 5885617.

22. Makhoul, J. "Linear Prediction: A Tutorial Review." *Proceedings of the IEEE*. 63 no. 4 (1975): 561–580. https://doi.org/10.1109/PROC.1975.9792. Bib-code:1975IEEEP..63..561M. ISSN 0018-9219.

23. Freedman, D.A. *Statistical Models: Theory and Practice* (Cambridge University Press, 2009), 26. ISBN 9780521743853.

24. Rosenblatt, Frank. *The Perceptron--A Perceiving and Recognizing Automaton*. Report 85-460-1, Cornell Aeronautical Laboratory, 1957.

25. Cortes, Corinna, Vladimir.N. Vapnik. "Support-Vector Networks." *Machine Learning*. 20 no. 3 (1995): 273–297. https://doi.org/10.1007/ BF00994018. CiteSeerX 10.1.1.15.9362.

26. McLachlan, G.J. *Discriminant Analysis and Statistical Pattern Recognition* (Wiley Interscience, 2004). ISBN 978-0-471-69115-0. MR 1190469.

27. Jolliffe I.T. "Principal Component Analysis, Series: Springer Series in Statistics." *Springer*, 2nd ed. (NY, 2002), XXIX, 487, 28 illus. ISBN 978-0-387-95442-4

28. https://www.amazon.com/s?k=wikipedia+the+free+encyclopedia&i=mobile-apps&adgrpid=1339205735248488&hvadid=83700747426985&hvbmt=be&hvdev=c&hvlocphy=66645&hvnetw=o&hvqmt=e&hvtargid=kwd-83700722718985%3Aloc-190&hydadcr=8416_13732460&msclkid=b2b694387935174509aef306d23da962&tag=mh0b-20&ref=pd_sl_6cojxxxez4_e.

29. Ciresan, D. and U. Meier, J. Schmidhuber. "Multi-Column Deep Neural Networks for Image Classification." 2012 IEEE Conference on Computer Vision and Pattern Recognition (2012): 3642–3649. https://doi.org/10.48550/arXiv.1202.2745 arXiv:1202.2745. ISBN 978-1-4673-1228-8. S2CID 2161592.

30. https://en.wikipedia.org/wiki/MNIST_database (Modified National Institute of Standards and Technology database.

31. https://en.wikipedia.org/wiki/Machine_learning#cite_note-2

32. https://towardsdatascience.com/parameters-and-hyperparameters-aa609601a9ac

33. https://deepchecks.com/training-validation-and-test-sets-what-are-the-differences/

34. [https://glassboxmedicine.com/2019/09/15/best-use-of-train-val-test-splits-with-tips-for-medical-data/#:~:text=Common%20ratios%20used%20are%3A,20%25%20val%2C%2020%25%20test]

35. https://deepchecks.com/training-validation-and-test-sets-what-are-the-differences/

36. Yang, Z.R. and Z. Yang. *Comprehensive Biomedical Physics* (Karolinska Institute, Stockholm, Sweden: Elsevier, 2014), 1. ISBN 978-0-444-53633-4.

37. https://en.wikipedia.org/wiki/Arthur_Samuel -Arthur Samuel (computer scientist)

38. https://community.anaconda.cloud/

39. https://docs.anaconda.com/free/anaconda/getting-started/what-is-distro/*

40. https://en.wikipedia.org/wiki/Project_Jupyter#Jupyter_Notebook

41. https://en.wikipedia.org/wiki/Python_(programming_language)

42. https://en.wikipedia.org/wiki/R_(programming_language)

43. https://en.wikipedia.org/wiki/Tableau_Software

44. https://en.wikipedia.org/wiki/Apache_Hadoop

45. Saleh, Hyatt. *Machine Learning Fundamentals: Use Python and Scikit-Learn to get up and Running With the Hottest Developments in Machine Learning* (Packt Publishing, 2018).

46. www.kdnuggets.com/2016/06/select-support-vector-machine-kernels.html.

47. www.kdnuggets.com/2016/04/deep-learning-vs-svm-random-forest.html.

48. Sahay, Amar. *Applied Regression and Modeling—A Computer Integrated Approach* (Business Expert Press, LLC, 222 East 46th Street, New York, NY 10017, n.d). ISBN: 13:978-63157-329-3.

49. MINITAB "Statistical Software"- www. minitab.com

50. https://en.wikipedia.org/wiki/Euclidean_distance#Squared_Euclidean _distance.

51. www.v7labs.com/blog/neural-networks-activation-functions.

52. Sahay, R., J. Stubbs, C. Brinton, and G. Birch. "An Uncertainty Quantification Framework for Counter Unmanned Aircraft Systems Using Deep Ensembles," *IEEE Sensors Journal* (2022).

53. Sahay, R., S. Appadwedula, D. Love, C. Brinton, "A Neural Network-Prepended GLRT Framework for Signal Detection Under Nonlinear Distortions," IEEE Communications Letters, 2022.

54. Sahay, R., C. Brinton, and D. Love. "A Deep Ensemble-Based Wireless Receiver Architecture for Mitigating Adversarial Attacks in Automatic Modulation Classification, *IEEE Transactions on Cognitive Communications and Networking*" (2021).

55. Sahay, R. and C. Brinton. "Robust Subject-Independent P300 Waveform Classification via Signal Pre-Processing and Deep Learning." *IEEE Access* (2021).

56. Sahay, A. *Essentials of Data Science and Analytics* (Business Expert Press, New York, 2021).

57. Sahay, A. *Business Analytics* (Business Expert Press, New York, 2020), 2 vols.

58. Kroese, D.P., Z.I. Botev, T. Taimre, R. Vaisman. *Data Science and Machine Learning: Mathematical and Statistical Methods* (Chapman and Hall/CRC, Boca Raton, 2019).

About the Authors

Author Biography: Rajeev Sahay

Dr. Rajeev Sahay is an Assistant Professor of Teaching in the Department of Electrical and Computer Engineering at UC San Diego. He received his Ph.D. and M.S. in 2022 and 2021, respectively, from the Elmore Family School of Electrical and Computer Engineering at Purdue University, and he received his B.S. in 2018 from the Department of Electrical and Computer Engineering at the University of Utah.

Dr. Sahay has significant teaching expereince in data science, machine learning, analog circuits, computer architecture, and programming languages in C, C++, and Python. Dr. Sahay's research interests lie in the intersection of machine learning and networking with applications in education and wireless communications. In the former, he is interested in developing machine learning approaches to promote social learning and personalized learning within and across classrooms and institutions while simultaneously preserving and protecting the privacy of student data. In the latter, he is interested in exploring the vulnerabilities of next-generation machine learning-based communications and developing robust signal processing algorithms capable of operating in hostile, crowded, and adversarial environments.

Author Biography: Amar Sahay

Dr. Amar Sahay is a professor engaged in teaching, research, consulting, and training. He has a BS in production engineering (BIT, India), an MS in industrial engineering, and a PhD in mechanical engineering—both from the University of Utah, USA. He has taught/teaching at several Utah institutions including the University of Utah (school of engineering and management), Weber State University, SLCC, Westminster College, and others. Amar is a certified Six Sigma master black belt and holds expertlevel certification in lean manufacturing/lean management.

He has over 30 research papers at national and international conferences. Amar is the author of 11 books in the areas of data visualization, business analytics, Six Sigma quality, statistics and data analysis, managing and improving quality, and applied regression. He is also associated with QMS Global—a company engaged in data visualization, analytics, Lean Six Sigma, manufacturing, and service systems research. Amar is a senior member of Industrial & Systems Engineers, American Society for Quality (ASQ), and Data Science (Data Science Central).

Some Related Books/Journal Papers by the Authors

Amar Sahay, A. *Business Analytics*, Vol. II (Business New York: Expert Press, New York, 2020).

Amar Sahay, A. *Essentials of Data Science and Analytics* (New York: Business Expert Press, New York, 2021).

Kroese, D.P., Z.I. Botev, T. Taimre, R. Vaisman. *Data Science and Machine Learning: Mathematical and Statistical Methods* (Boca Raton: Chapman and Hall/CRC, Boca Raton, 2019).

Sahay, R. and C. Brinton. "Robust Subject-Independent P300 Waveform Classification via Signal Pre-Processing and Deep Learning," *IEEE Access*.

Sahay, R. C. Brinton, D. Love, "A Deep Ensemble-Based Wireless Receiver Architecture for Mitigating Adversarial Attacks in Automatic Modulation Classification," *IEEE Transactions on Cognitive Communications and Networking*.

Sahay, R., J. Stubbs, C. Brinton, G. Birch. "An Uncertainty Quantification Framework for Counter Unmanned Aircraft Systems Using Deep Ensembles," *IEEE Sensors Journal*.

Sahay, R., S. Appadwedula, D. Love, C. Brinton. "A Neural Network-prepended GLRT Framework for Signal Detection under Nonlinear Distortions," *IEEE Communications Letters*.

Index

OTHER TITLES IN THE BIG DATA, BUSINESS ANALYTICS, AND SMART TECHNOLOGY COLLECTION

Mark Ferguson, University of South Carolina, Editor

- *Cracking the Data Code* by Richard C. Robinson
- *Digital Leadership Framework* by Amit Prabhu
- *Digital Strategy Framework* by Amit Prabhu
- *Thriving in a Data World* by Sangeeta Krishnan
- *Business Models in Emerging Technologies* by Stylianos Kampakis, Theodosis Mourouzis, Marialena Zinopoulou and Gerard Cardoso
- *Getting Data Science Done* by John Hawkins
- *Four Laws for the Artificially Intelligent* by Ian Domowitz
- *The Data Mirage* by Ruben Ugarte
- *Introduction to Business Analytics, Second Edition* by Majid Nabavi, David L. Olson and Wesley S. Boyce
- *Emerging Technologies* by Errol S. van Engelen
- *Data-Driven Business Models for the Digital Economy* by Rado Kotorov
- *Highly Effective Marketing Analytics* by Mu Hu

Concise and Applied Business Books

The Collection listed above is one of 30 business subject collections that Business Expert Press has grown to make BEP a premiere publisher of print and digital books. Our concise and applied books are for...

- Professionals and Practitioners
- Faculty who adopt our books for courses
- Librarians who know that BEP's Digital Libraries are a unique way to offer students ebooks to download, not restricted with any digital rights management
- Executive Training Course Leaders
- Business Seminar Organizers

Business Expert Press books are for anyone who needs to dig deeper on business ideas, goals, and solutions to everyday problems. Whether one print book, one ebook, or buying a digital library of 110 ebooks, we remain the affordable and smart way to be business smart. For more information, please visit www.businessexpertpress.com, or contact sales@businessexpertpress.com.